T0358540

Routledge Library Editions

PROBLEMS OF
ECONOMIC PLANNING

ECONOMICS

PUBLIC ECONOMICS
In 5 Volumes

PROBLEMS OF ECONOMIC PLANNING

Papers on Planning and Economics

E F M DURBIN

LONDON AND NEW YORK

First published in 1949

Reprinted in 2003 by
Routledge
2 Park Square, Milton Park, Abingdon, Oxon OX14 4RN

Transferred to Digital Printing 2004

Routledge is an imprint of the Taylor & Francis Group

Printed and Bound in Great Britain

British Library Cataloguing in Publication Data
A CIP catalogue record for this book
is available from the British Library

Problems of Economic Planning
ISBN 0-415-31398-8

Miniset: Public Economics

Series: Routledge Library Editions – Economics

Printed and bound by Antony Rowe Ltd, Eastbourne

Problems of ECONOMIC PLANNING

PAPERS ON PLANNING AND ECONOMICS

by

E. F. M. DURBIN

With a Foreword by
The Right Honourable CLEMENT R. ATTLEE, M.P.

LONDON
ROUTLEDGE & KEGAN PAUL LIMITED
BROADWAY HOUSE: 68–74 CARTER LANE, E.C.4

First published 1949

PRINTED IN GREAT BRITAIN
BY HUNT, BARNARD AND COMPANY LTD., LONDON AND AYLESBURY

CONTENTS

ACKNOWLEDGMENTS

This book contains a number of articles that, with one exception, have been published before. The details of previous publications are as follows:

1. The Case for Socialism—Chapters III and VI of my *What Have We to Defend?* published by Messrs. Routledge in 1942.

2. Democracy and Socialism in Great Britain—*Political Quarterly* for 1935.

3. The Importance of Planning—Chapter IX of *New Trends in Socialism* edited by Professor Catlin and published by Messrs. Lovat Dickson in 1935.

5. Professor Hayek on Economic Planning—*Economic Journal* for 1945.

6. Government Administration and Efficiency—*Political Quarterly* for 1944.

7. Social Significance of the Theory of Value—*Economic Journal* for 1935.

8. Economic Calculations in a Planned Economy—*Economic Journal* for 1936.

9. The Nature of Economics—Chapter XII of *Economics: Man and his Material Resources,* published by Odhams' Press in 1949.

10. Methods of Research—*Economic Journal* for 1938.

11. Economists and the Future Functions of the State—*Political Quarterly* for 1943.

I am indebted to Messrs. Macmillans for permission to re-publish papers from the *Political Quarterly* and the *Economic Journal,* to Odhams' Press for permission to re-publish my Chapter from *Economics: Man and his Material Resources,* and to Messrs. Lovat Dickson for permission to re-publish my contribution to *New Trends in Socialism.* I should like to express my gratitude to them.

FOREWORD

AN APPRECIATION OF E. F. M. DURBIN

BY THE RT. HON. C. R. ATTLEE

THE tragic death of Evan Durbin at the early age of forty-two deprived the nation and especially the Labour and Socialist Movement of a man of great distinction of mind and character who might well have given service for many years.

Without any advantage of wealth, beginning his education in the elementary school he won scholarships which took him to Oxford where he had a brilliant academic career. As a lecturer at Oxford and at the London School of Economics he proved an admirable and inspiring teacher. He was accounted one of the ablest of the younger economists, but he was no abstract theorist. During the war years he did good service in the Cabinet secretariat and for a time was my personal assistant. He gained a practical knowledge of administration which served him well when in 1945 he entered Parliament. It was obvious to all that he would not stay long on the back benches and at the time of his death he was doing very well as Parliamentary Secretary in the Ministry of Works. There is no doubt that had he lived he would have gone far.

But his great intellectual gifts were allied to a singularly modest and unselfish nature. It was altogether characteristic of him that he should have lost his life while saving others. His life was inspired by a noble idealism. A convinced Socialist and tenacious of his opinions, he had a wide toleration and remained on terms of friendship with those who disputed his conclusions.

He had during the last nine years written many articles and books on economic and political subjects. The most outstanding of these was his book on The Politics of Democratic Socialism published in 1942. Everyone in the British Labour and Socialist Movement and indeed democratic socialists in other lands are indebted to him for this forceful and clear exposition of the faith that was in him. He did a service in showing clearly the way that should be followed, confuting alike the upholders of Russian Communism and capitalism.

He had hoped to have followed this with a companion volume on the Economics of Democratic Socialism. That hope has proved vain, but in the present volume is collected a number of essays which make a valuable contribution to the solution of some of the problems which present themselves in the changing conditions of the present day.

I believe that some of his writings will have an enduring place in social and economic literature. I am certain that the memory of his lovable personality and the example which he set of high aims and intellectual integrity will be cherished by his many friends for long years.

I was privileged to enjoy his friendship and honoured to have had his help.

C. R. ATTLEE.

INTRODUCTION

WHEN I published my book on the *Politics of Democratic Socialism* in 1940, I hoped and intended to write a companion volume—*The Economics of Democratic Socialism* as soon as I was released from full-time employment in the Civil Service. But the result of the General Election of 1945 involved me, first as a Member of Parliament and then as a Junior Minister, in the practice of these policies instead of their exposition. I must therefore postpone the book once more for two reasons—first because there is no time to write it, and secondly because there is much to be learned from the new evidence that is now accumulating swiftly. Sometime in the future, however, the time will come (and perhaps the opportunity) to write it.

In the meantime I have decided to re-publish a number of papers I wrote for the "learned journals", and the parts of books to which I have contributed during the last fifteen years, that bear upon the problems of economic planning in a free society. The resulting book is inevitably unsystematic and incomplete, though the various parts of it are connected by a common theme and a common purpose. My reasons for allowing the book to go forward are that I have been pressed by a number of people to do so, and the literature on the subject is certainly not extensive. I can only hope that some readers will find the book useful.

The "Papers" fall into three groups. The first four attempt to explain the idea of "socialism" and define its relation to democracy. Part II—the main part of the book—contains six papers on various problems of economic planning. Of these four are concerned with political economy on the practice of planning, and the last two with the application of the traditional theory of value to the conditions of a centrally directed economy. The last group of three papers discusses the nature of economics. The papers are re-printed as first published, but I have added explanatory notes at the beginning of all of them.

1*

Introduction

I should like to express my gratitude to those of my late colleagues at the London School of Economics, particularly Professor Robbins and Professor Hayek, who, by criticising and disagreeing with almost everything I have ever said about this subject, have kept me thinking about it.

E. F. M. D.

THE MEANING OF SOCIALISM

THE CASE FOR SOCIALISM

Four National Faults

This Paper consists of two passages (Chapters III and VI) from my little book "What Have We to Defend?" (now out of print), written during the war in ". . . an attempt to explain why a pacific international socialist feels it necessary to support the war". During the course of my argument I contended that despite the obvious faults in the British social system it was "one of the finest that men had yet built for themselves" and not the least important of its virtues lay in the fact that ". . . it contains, more certainly than any other, the means for its own improvement". The relevance of these passages to the subject of this book lies in these two propositions. An analysis of the roots of inequality and inefficiency in our pre-war society constitutes the main practical reason for seeking to change it—while the last step in the argument makes plain the inherence of political democracy in the British conception of socialism. Certain phrases I have used spring from the higher emotional tension of war-time and do not fit the pedestrian mood of a difficult peace, but I have thought it better to leave the text unchanged.

L ET us begin with the debit side of the account. It would be idle to pretend that in defending this country we are defending a perfect society. We have not yet created a social paradise and we do our cause no service by closing our eyes to our own faults, since we shall not be able, when the time comes, to improve our heritage if we have not understood the exact respects in which the nation has fallen short of a practicable ideal.

It is scarcely necessary to point out that these are matters of personal opinion, but I shall argue that there are at least four ways in which our habits and institutions offend, unnecessarily, against attainable standards of justice and good sense—in the distribution of wealth, in the division of our people into social classes, in the growth of modern vandalism and by the limitation in the understanding and imagination of our people. I do not say that these are our only, or indeed our worst shortcomings, but they are sufficiently outstanding to merit attention.

Let us look for a moment at each of them.

I. Economic Inequality

The distribution of income and property is amazingly unequal in this country.

The most recent investigations suggest that 10 per cent of the population receive over 45 per cent of the national money income, while 90 per cent receive the remaining 55 per cent. The distribution of property is even more unequal. 1 per cent of the population own 60 per cent of the saleable assets of the nation. It is still almost true to say, and it is only a short time since it was quite true to say, that 10 per cent of the people owned 90 per cent of the property, and 90 per cent of the people owned 10 per cent of the property. Individual incomes range from £1,000,000 a year to £50 per year—a range of 20,000-fold or 2,000,000 per cent. [1]

It is true that the degree of distributive inequality is even greater in other countries (India, for example), and that all the evidence goes to show that it is slowly diminishing here; but the extraordinary extent to which it still persists is an instant challenge to most men's instinctive sense of justice. Could such a method of showing the fruits of our common labour ever be justified?

To answer this question satisfactorily it is necessary to understand one reason for the present distribution of wealth. It can be shown that this extreme degree of inequality is due to the right of *inheritance* at present vested in the legal institution of property. [2] Large individual fortunes are, for the most part, made up of inherited property. The rich, as a class, are *born* with silver spoons in their mouths and the economic privileges that they enjoy were not acquired by the possession or exercise of great talents, but by the accident of birth. Their position as a group is maintained and strengthened because wealthy

---

[1] Colin Clark, *National Income and Outlay*, and Daniels and Campion, *The Distribution of Property*.
[2] Dalton, *Inequality of Income*.

people are better able to add to their capital by saving and find it easier to enter the highly paid professions since these latter occupations are necessarily hedged about with long and expensive periods of training. Hence the present right to pass wealth from generation to generation accounts directly for the unequal distribution of property and unearned incomes; and indirectly for a large part of the differences in earned income. The rich have it both ways.

It follows from this account of the matter that the abolition of inheritance (gradual or swift) would strike at the foundation of economic inequality even if the other rights of property were left intact.

But it would be foolish to suppose that no respectable defence had ever been offered for a legal arrangement that is characteristic of most stable societies and has been continuously supported by intelligent men of goodwill. Three arguments have chiefly been used to maintain the view that property and inheritance are essential institutions in a healthy and developing community—namely, that the possibility of gaining larger incomes is a necessary incentive to individual efficiency; that the inheritance of property is a natural right of, and a necessary basis for, the family; that the existence of very rich people will guarantee a high rate of economic progress.

These arguments are of very different merit.

The *first* of them offers, I would suggest, no adequate justification for *inheritance*. It may be true that the provision, by society, of larger incomes to those who work harder, or possess rare qualities in a high degree is an obvious, and perhaps indispensable, method of securing the greatest possible development, and wisest utilisation, of these necessary services. And it may, moreover, be wise to allow the instinctive impulse to accumulate a reserve of property against a "rainy day" a certain opportunity to develop and fulfil itself. But these considerations do not, I feel, provide a reason for permitting the wealth, built up in a lifetime, to pass, in a growing sequence, from generation to generation. Such an arrangement provides no certain incentive to efficiency. Those who bequeath property, may, it is true, find an added impulse to labour and save in the thought that their children and grandchildren will benefit from their industry and thrift. But no motive of this kind can arise in the minds of those who *receive* such an inheritance. Indeed, precisely the opposite consequence is likely to follow. In so far as economic necessity provides a reason for harder work and greater saving, the passive acquisition of unearned income at birth will reduce for the lifetime of the recipient the constraints of poverty and need. The net result of inheritance may therefore be a reduction in the efficacy of economic incentives (since the thought of providing income for future generations is only one of many motives for acquisitiveness, while the possession of income removes all of them) and the legal institution of bequest is not therefore defensible, in my view, upon this first ground.

But, in the *second* place, it may be held that the power of bequest is a price that must be paid for the maintenance of the family as an institution. It is some notion of this kind that must lie behind the conception that bequest is a "natural right", and a cause of social order. Although this idea is not simple or obvious it would be folly to deny that it exerts a great influence upon the public mind.

This is a difficult and uncertain subject and it is unwise to be dogmatic. Nevertheless I find it difficult to accept this argument or to escape the conclusion that it arises from a confusion of cause and effect. Inheritance, as we know it, is normally associated with the family, but that is surely because family affection provides the main reason for bequest and not that inheritance is the main reason for family affection? The family existed long before the right of inheritance—it exists to-day in societies still too primitive to possess any detailed law of personal property—and, as we have seen, the great majority of parents have little or nothing to leave their children even in a relatively rich community like our own. Can it be argued that the family, as an institution, is less closely bound and less stable among the poor than among the rich? The statistics of divorce would certainly provide no justification for such view. They would show that among the rich, divorce is more frequent than among the poor, and, although this is partly due to the expense of legal proceedings, it is a plain indication that property is no guarantee of a successful marriage and happy family life. In so far as they are causally related, is not the family the cause of (or reason for) inheritance and not the other way about? It would seem more reasonable to think so.

The most weighty argument for inheritance is to be found, in my view, in the *third* of the reasons enumerated above—in the contention that inheritance is the simplest and least costly method of securing a high rate of economic progress and a rapid rise in the general standard of living.

The argument is familiar to economists. The inheritance of property is the chief cause of inequality in the distribution of wealth. One consequence of inequality is the existence of a group of very rich persons commanding the services of a large proportion of the national resources. Now the rich are *able* to save a larger fraction of their incomes than the poor and it is therefore to be expected that a high degree of inequality will be associated with a high rate of saving. As long as the money made available by the rich is all used to finance the construction of new physical capital (more efficient instruments of production) the pace of economic development will be great and the real goods available for consumption (upon which alone an increasing standard of living can be based) will increase at a relatively rapid rate. Inequality will result in prosperity—and distributive injustice will be offset by productive efficiency.

It is obvious that this is an important consideration. If it were true that the wealth of the rich will slowly improve the wages of the poor and that the poor would be poorer if the rich were less rich, then it would be right to admit that inequality of wealth and opportunity was not an unmixed evil. And there is a great deal of evidence to show that this theory did apply with great force to certain periods of history and, in particular, to the earlier stages of capitalist development. In this country it can be demonstrated that the construction of the first great stocks of machinery (a process commonly known as "the "Industrial Revolution") was largely financed out of the savings of the wealthy merchants who had taken part in the imperial commerce of the seventeenth and eighteenth centuries. This association of the rich with saving and with industrial expansion continued throughout the nineteenth century and lasted until the outbreak of the European War in 1914. During this period it is not inaccurate to say that the savings of the rich contributed largely to the diminishing economic misery of the poor. It does not follow that inequality in that degree

7

was justified by this consequence, but it would be wrong to deny that the tree of inequality did, at this time, bear desirable fruit. [1]

It is by this argument that many men who care for social equity and the fate of the poor, have justified to themselves the maintenance of the right of bequest despite the extreme differences of wealth to which it obviously leads. Needless to say, the reasoning that has been used by honest men has been misused by those, less honest, who care only to preserve the privileges conferred upon them by the lottery of birth.

But, for good or evil, the argument has ceased to possess weight or validity. It can be shown that the rich have, in recent years, ceased to make any important contribution to the savings of the nation. Mr. Clark calculates [2] that in the fifteen years before 1935 the rich, as a class, *saved nothing at all*. Certain rich people added to their wealth by the purchase of securities, but this saving by one set of persons was offset, and probably more than offset, by the sale of securities (largely, no doubt, to pay death duties) by another group of individuals—making the net saving of the super-tax-paying class equal to zero. [3]

Precisely the same result can be obtained from an examination of the sources from which saving did flow. It can be shown that the savings of the poor (gathered through the Savings Banks, Co-operative, Industrial and Friendly Societies) together with the contributions of the middle class to insurance and endowment policies, and the undistributed profits added to company reserves, amount between them to a total as great as the whole amount invested in the construction of new capital. It will be noticed, therefore, that the whole of our national capital accumulation has recently been financed without receiving any contribution from the owners of large

[1] It will be particularly obvious to economists that a high rate of capital accumulation (produced by inequality) does not justify the inequality itself, since there are other ways of bringing about this result. Capital accumulation can be financed by the State. It therefore follows that, although inequality can and does produce increasing prosperity at certain times, it is not a *necessary* condition and cannot therefore be adduced as a justification for distributive injustice. If we can go up a mountain by a road or a railway it is no justification for climbing by the road to say that it leads up the mountain—it may be better to go up by train.

[2] Cf. *National Income and Outlay.*

[3] Or, to put the same point in another way, the savings of some rich men have been used to buy the securities sold by other rich men, so that rich men, as a group, have made no saving available to industry.

incomes. The increase in the height of all direct taxes—income tax, super-tax and death duties—has made the rich unwilling to maintain their saving at the expense of their standard of living. They have preferred personal comfort to social utility—but this chosen alternative carries with it a certain nemesis.

This recent change in the sources of saving affects profoundly the argument about economic inequality. Inequality is largely due to inheritance and one reason for the maintenance of this right lay in the expectation that it would lead, through the thrift of the very rich, to a high rate of capital accumulation. But this is no longer the case. Inheritance and inequality do not now lead to prosperity because the rich do not save.

There is then, in my opinion, no good economic reason for maintaining the right of inheritance. It provides no clear incentive to personal efficiency; it is not necessary to the preservation of the family; and it now contributes nothing to the funds required to finance economic progress. Yet it is accompanied by great financial inequality. The splendour of the rich has become parasitic and serves no useful social purpose. Inequality of educational opportunity and the closure of all expensive careers—law, medicine, the arts and the sciences—to those blessed only with talent, wastes an intolerable amount of the intelligence and vitality of the nation. Economic injustice is at once both wasteful and shameful—it is the relic of an institution that once served a valuable purpose but which has now outlived its usefulness and remains a dangerous survival, dividing us from each other and marring the justice of our free society. [1]

II. Social Inequality

We are a snobbish people. It is a paradox of our national tradition that we combine so great a political liberty with so much social subservience. No other great country in the world

[1]It is perhaps right to point out:

(*a*) that I am merely expressing my own views in this section and that there are many economists who would not agree with my final interpretation of the facts;

(*b*) that there are other *political* arguments which I have not examined, e.g., that the existence of the rich provides us with an independent public-spirited governing class or a necessary stabilising influence in society.

It is impossible in a short book to deal systematically with the whole problem and I have been content to express my personal judgment on the arguments that I believe have influenced democratic opinion.

provides more freedom of thought and speech or offers its citizens a larger share in the work of government. Yet in no other literate community is there more respect for the mediæval paraphernalia of title and class, birth and gentlemanly breeding. No other modern state has preserved a purely hereditary Second Chamber—our incomparable House of Lords!

The apparatus of social hierarchy in this country is amazingly complete. It is manifest in the Court with its great expense and elaborate (if dignified) display; the country house with its ancient associations and dependent village; the segregation of a group of schools (ironically called "public" schools) to provide each new generation with the manners and habits of a ruling class; the clubs and social life of London; the columns of "Society" gossip in the newspapers and the differences of clothing and accent by which members of the "classes" can instantly recognise one another. The system is so ingrained, and the subservience so natural and unconscious, that an old and dignified countryman rich in years and wisdom will, without a moment's thought or embarrassment, touch his cap and say "Good day, *sir*," to any passing young man who wears the right clothes and greets him with the right accent!

This extraordinary preservation (although on a diminishing scale) of symbolic class differences is open to a number of misinterpretations. It does not mean, for example, as the political intellectual of the Left always assumes, a feeling of dependence or hatred or fear on the part of the "working" classes. In this country, almost alone among the hierarchical societies of the world, the relationship between the rich and aristocratic on the one hand, the poor and humble on the other, is predominantly one of mutual respect. There are, of course, an immense number of individual exceptions to this rule— many rich men (especially if they are not well born) are justly hated by the poor. But, for the greater part, an Englishman (and an English woman) still loves a lord—and most lords respond in kind. The penny newspapers are full of the (frequently trivial and silly) doings of the rich, not (in my view) because the newspapers are the instruments of a subtle class tyranny, but because the common man, and more particularly the common woman, is interested in the life of the strange and remote world in which the wealthy live and of which she may feel some distant envy but for which she feels no hatred whatever.

This feeling of distance and curiosity, tolerance and respect, between rich and poor is one of the controlling forces in our recent history. It has taken the sting out of the struggle between the privileged and the dispossessed. It has muted the strings of social discord and bound the nation more closely together in its common mood of slow and conservative reform.

I am not, however, concerned with the causes or the consequences of the relationship between our social classes, but with the ethical nature of voluntary class subordination—with the value of snobbishness as such.

Can there be any doubt that this characteristic feeling of ours is a moral weakness (however amiable) and offensive to our dignity as human beings?

There is no virtue in wealth or in the accident of birth. We should respect our fellow creatures because they are good or clever, gifted or wise—not because they happen to possess advantages of wealth or power. It is cowardly and undignified to pay respect where none is due; to accept the leadership of those who are not qualified to lead.

In so far as we accept these false standards (of wealth and class) we make ourselves less than free men. We deny the equality of our common humanity.

It is not, of course, that men and women are born physically, intellectually or spiritually equal. They differ in every conceivable way—in brains, in skill, in sensibility and in moral control—some can play tennis and others football, some are kind and others cruel, some are simple and all are sinful. The great mass of us are not very clever, or very good at games, or very kind or even very wicked. It is only a tiny minority of the human race that can do anything particularly well—Shakespeares and Newtons and Gladstones are rarities—and it is natural that we should look up to men and women of great ability or great virtue. But respect should be for persons and not for classes. There is nothing shameful in acknowledging and admiring the superiority of Einstein in mathematics, of Cochet in tennis, of Bach in the art of musical composition, of Charlie Chaplin's clowning, of Winston Churchill's oratory and leadership. These are great men, each in his own way made for the admiration of the world. But there is something shameful in mistaking the form for the substance—in bowing down before clothes and accents, in accepting the presumptuous superiority, based upon injustice, of class distinctions.

Again, let us be careful to think clearly and not to exaggerate our national faults. There is something natural and inevitable in the respect we feel for those who carry in their veins, through the continuity of inheritance, the blood of the great men and women of the past. It would be unnatural if we were not moved to interest and respect if we met the lineal descendant of Shakespeare or Darwin, Jane Austen or Madame Curie, Queen Elizabeth or Abraham Lincoln, Hobbs or Bradman; and it would be unnatural if we felt no curiosity in meeting the offspring of great and wicked men like Napoleon or Henry VIII, Hitler or Ivan the Terrible. These men and women were, for good or ill, *great*. They possessed remarkable powers, they could do difficult things, they stand above the stature of ordinary human beings. And although very gifted people rarely have children of equal greatness with themselves, there is enough substance in the principle of heredity to lead us to expect that the descendants of remarkable people will possess power above the average of their fellows. It is, therefore, inevitable that we, ordinary mortals, should feel curious about the present representatives of the families from which the great men and women of our past history sprang. This is not snobbishness but an instinctive and scientifically grounded respect for the principle of heredity.

But this sensible curiosity does not justify snobbishness. Snobbishness is undiscriminating and unscientific. It is respect for a class—for the empty signs of wealth and breeding. When my kindly and dignified ploughman touches his cap and says "sir" to a passing stranger he is not acknowledging a respect for heredity. He does not even know the name and family of the passer-by: he is simply accepting, by force of habit, his subordinate position in a system of social classes and acknowledging the outward symbols of money and education—gifts that may be acquired by the offspring of the most wicked or the dullest of God's creatures. He humiliates himself unnecessarily in the service of a dangerous superstition—that one man is better than another because he is richer, cleverer or more aristocratic—and bows his knee to false gods of hierarchy and power.

From this false worship we should, as a nation, turn away in shame and accept, instead, the responsible judgment and difficult challenge of human equality.

We are all men, born in weakness, heirs to the same vices, capable of the same courage and kindness, prey to the same diseases, bound for the same unseen goal. We need neither bow down to one another in unthinking subjection nor pride ourselves on our passing honours. We all lay helpless in the cradle once and we shall all lie together within the earth soon enough. The things we share in common are so much more important and terrible than the trifles that separate us into classes. Let us, by all means, pay proper respect to the great and the clever; but let us root out of our hearts the snobbish love of a social hierarchy founded neither upon service nor excellence. Let us greet one another as friends walking together upon a difficult and dangerous but surprisingly interesting pathway—a common journey that leaves us no time to ask which of us came from Mayfair and which from Shoreditch.

III. Vandalism

To me the worst vice, because the most senseless, peculiar to our own time has been the destructive vandalism with which we have treated our physical heritage in town and country. The period between the two European wars will stand out as one of the most destructive epochs in our history—a rival to the plundering neglect of the Tudors and the savagery of the Puritans.

The land is strewn with the wreckage of what was once beautiful. Hitler's bombers have not yet wrought one-tenth of the æsthetic damage that we carefully accomplished ourselves, with full legal sanction, in the years before the war began. We have fouled our own nest and spat upon our own altars.

Neither town nor countryside escaped. In London almost everything pleasant has been torn to pieces and the more beautiful a building dared to look the more certain it was that men would come with picks and cranes and drills to break it into pieces. The uniform brick and stucco squares, for which

London has been justly famous throughout the world, and in whose midst trees and grass stirred a nostalgic memory of the distant countryside, were violated and mangled. The pleasant houses have been destroyed and replaced by buildings of different heights, discordant designs and clashing materials. New and garish brick stands next to steel and concrete, and in some particularly horrible cases to green and yellow tiles; while here and there remains in the midst of the nightmare, dignified but forlorn, a relic of the old harmony.

Nor have the streets been any more fortunate—Regent Street, Portland Place, Adelphi Terrace, Park Lane, have been replaced by a jumble of disparate and incongruous palaces of cement and steel; and even the solitary "processional way" in this great capital city (Carlton House Terrace) is now overtopped and spoiled by a jarring excrescence—a desecration that the indignation of Crown and Parliament combined appeared too feeble to prevent.

All this architectural savagery is quite senseless. It is perfectly possible to adapt old buildings to new purposes, or to reconstruct the interiors behind a uniform front; or, if preservation is impossible, to rebuild a large area as an harmonious whole. All the new building in London is not ugly or disastrous. When a good architect has been employed and a large area has been planned as a unit (the only example of this happy combination that occurs to me is the new building of the University of London in Bloomsbury) the result has been to replace the quiet charm of one age with the greater strength of another. In certain areas squalor has been replaced by cleanness (the buildings on each side of Euston Road are a case in point). But these are the exceptions to a depressingly general rule. We have for the most part carelessly destroyed what did not belong to us—the beauty of old things left to our charge and held in trust for the future.

The solution was obvious to all but the blind and those who profited from the loot. Certain areas (such as the south bank of the river and all the approaches to the City) should have been scheduled for reconstruction and rebuilt in districts, while other parts of London (the better squares in Bloomsbury, Mayfair, Belgravia and Chelsea, and the environs of the large parks) should have been scheduled for preservation and adaptation behind the existing façades. By this simple means we could have had the best of both worlds—combining the efficiency and comfort of modern interiors with the charming exteriors of earlier centuries—and we should have seen a London grow more beautiful about us every year; a record of the richest achievements of every age including our own. Instead we have chosen to deface and to desecrate—with the carelessness and fear of little men.

No other civilised people could have been guilty of so wretched a record.

The evil we have done in London (and in other towns) pales into insignificance in my mind before the insensate wickedness with which we have ravaged the countryside of southern England. We have inherited in these little islands one of the richest and most varied treasure houses in the world. God and man have worked together for centuries to produce a gallery of perfect paintings—from the softness of the Weald to the harder greens and blues of Skye, from the clear emptiness of the Fens to the manifold luxury of the estuaries of Merionethshire and Devon. To this incomparable inheritance the southern half of England had much to contribute—the meadows of the Thames, the wooded downs of Sussex, the ancient stones of Purbeck, the grey, grass-crowned bastions of Cornwall, the oak-wooded valleys of Exmoor, the ascetic calm of the Wiltshire chalk, and the splendour of the Chiltern beeches curving over the little hills.

Upon this lovely body we have allowed the speculative builder to fall in a ferocious rape. He was allowed and encouraged to spoil mile after mile of the most beautiful countryside in the world—the North Downs have been ruined, the South Downs are in danger, the whole southern coast of England (with the exception of certain stretches in Dorsetshire protected by large landowners) has been irreparably spoiled, the Chilterns have been destroyed, Oxford has been desecrated, the Cotswolds are threatened; and, worst of all, no view in England (however lovely), or site (however soaked in the history and genius of our race), is really safe (apart from a tiny number held by the National Trust). At any moment some thoughtless or selfish person, indifferent to the thing he destroys, or seeking to possess it for himself alone, is free to erect a pimple of brick or concrete or corrugated iron in the midst of it—bungalows breaking the skyline of the Wiltshire downs, tin shacks squatting in the remote coves of Devonshire, Peacehaven upon the cliffs of Sussex, Woolworth's in the Cathedral Close, road-houses in the Chiltern valleys—a riot of ruthless, moronish vandalism. We have treated our land as though we hated it.

In point of fact the crime has been made possible more by stupidity than by wickedness. It is extraordinary that the Conservatives, who were in power for nineteen out of the twenty-one years that elapsed between the two wars, and who were supposed to care for all that was valuable in our social heritage, should have done nothing effective to preserve the main physical part of it. What culpable stupidity it has been! Three-quarters of the damage could have been avoided without diminishing the national housing programme by a single jerrybuilt villa. We must, of course, have houses—and yet more houses. One of the greatest achievements of the twenties and thirties of this century has been the improvement in the housing standards of a large part of our population, and this improvement must continue as rapidly after this war as it did before it. But if the location of new building were properly controlled there would be nothing to fear from the growth of building. The largest number of houses that we shall ever need can only occupy a small percentage of the space in which they would do no æsthetic harm. Position is the vital factor. Let me give two examples of what I mean—a small and a large one:

1 I know a case where a vandal built a house for use at week-ends and holidays in the Sussex Downs. He built it within a mile of an existing village but he chose a site upon the skyline of a smooth breast of grassland from which it could be seen for miles around—breaking the perfect symmetry of the chalk with a wound. Only a mile away, on the outskirts of the existing village, the house would not have been noticed at all—it would have been no more beautiful in that position but it would have been incomparably less conspicuous. The house was built on the hill in order that the owner might enjoy, without walking a mile, the loveliness of the downland folds and the distant prospect of the sea; but in order to achieve this purpose he destroyed the thing he sought to possess and hid it

from every eye except his own. This was an anti-social crime of great selfishness and it should have been prevented by law.

2 At the opposite extreme of size stands the stupidity exhibited in the suburban development of London. In the years following the 1914 war London grew and spread enormously. The growth was inevitable and the spread was necessary in order to satisfy the Englishman's longing for a garden of his own. But the direction and location of the new housing was short-sighted and wasteful in the extreme. London was situated a few miles north of some beautiful chalk country—the Surrey Downs. It possessed to the east and north-east the plains of Essex, and in the north-east, the north and the north-west the pleasant rolling country of Hertfordshire and to the west the plains of Middlesex. All this latter country, with the exception of a few marshy tracts in Middlesex, is perfectly suitable for suburban development—dry and healthy soil. Yet instead of building out in these harmless directions the people and housing were allowed to creep in a plague over the whole of the southern chalk. This was a process of inevitable self-frustration—each individual moved into Surrey in the hope and expectation of enjoying precisely those advantages that the movement, on a communal scale, destroyed. The final result is the worst possible muddle—the lunatic consequence of social unreason—the good country that all could enjoy is blotted by settlers who gain nothing from what they have destroyed, while the land to the north, at which no one particularly wishes to look but which is as good as any other for suburban life, stands empty. Something of inestimable value has been thoughtlessly killed and no one has gained from the murder.

This destructiveness must be checked. It is too late to save large parts of London and Oxford. It is too late to save the North Downs; the coast-line of Kent and Sussex, of South Devon and Cornwall; the Chilterns and the lower valley of the Thames. These beautiful things are gone for ever and we can only curse the memory of our fathers who let them go. But there is much, so much to save—the Isle of Purbeck, the north coast of Devon and Cornwall, the valleys and moors of the Dart and the Exe, the plain of Somerset, the Cotswolds, the little mountains of Breconshire and Merioneth, Snowdonia, the hills of Salop, the Yorkshire dales and wolds, all Cumberland and

17

Westmorland, the grassy fastnesses of the Cheviots, and the unparalleled beauty of the Western Islands and Highlands of Scotland. There are even a few towns that might be saved from the wreckage—Cambridge, York and Edinburgh; Stamford, Lincoln and Chester; the villages of Suffolk and Gloucestershire; Rye, Dunster and Turville—and a hundred more. We have shamefully wasted our substance but we are not bankrupt yet. We have wealth beyond counting—beauty beyond comparison—the fruit of a thousand years of loving care—if only we will awake from our sleep, tragic in its fruits, and snatch our heritage from the hands of the despoiler.

IV. Lack of Imagination

We are not a stupid people, but we are very unimaginative. Many of our vices—and some of our virtues—can be traced to this one root cause.

Imagination is the power to see what is not there, to experience what has not yet come to be, to walk in the past or in the future. The English people have little time for visions, they have no leisure in which to dream. Their feet are planted firmly upon the ground and they are content to overcome the difficulties of to-day.

It would be foolish to pretend that this quality of the British character has no advantages. A lack of imagination helps English people to maintain the physical courage they possess in such a high degree. Unimaginativeness is not essential to bravery—many imaginative people are brave despite the power of their inner minds to picture the horror that does not yet exist, and a large number of very stupid and wholly unfanciful people run away at the first smell of danger. But a weak imagination does make it easier to be brave. It is difficult enough to face real dangers, but those who can see into the future starve long before the ships have been sunk and die a hundred times before the bombs begin to fall. Such people bear a heavier burden and find it more difficult to keep their courage in a war.

Bravery is a precious thing. In a world of international anarchy it is a virtue without which all other gifts are of little use. It is no good to be clever if you have to argue with a gangster and a machine-gun. Sensibility will not protect us if and when the Germans invade our islands. Even kindliness is not sufficient if it leads to slavery. As the bombs come whistling through the air, as old women are buried beneath piles of bricks and tiles, as torpedoes blow out the bottoms of our merchant ships, let us be thankful for any deficiency that helps to sustain the magnificent calm, the steadfast fatalism, and the cheerfulness of our people.

There is a second great advantage that is partly derived from the unimaginative nature of the ordinary Englishman—his lack of interest in comprehensive systems of thought. He is not swept off his feet by theories—political or philosophical. His mind does not rest upon any system of abstractions and he is not therefore the victim of fashionable theories or the hysteria of intellectual groups. His mind is both pedestrian and scientific —his feet are firmly planted and he tests generalisation by the safe standards of experience and practicability. "Will it account for my experience on the Town Council?—Would it work in the business of the Urban District Council of Muggle-town-on-Sea?" These are the first questions asked about any political or social theory and the final evidence by which it is judged. It is for this reason, among others, that extreme doctrine has had so little success in this country—why the Marxist theory has never captured any mass movement. It accounts for the intellectual stability, the slow development of thought, the continuity of the British political tradition—all valuable things. France might not have fallen if her people had not possessed so sensitive an imagination.

But we pay too high a price—far too high a price—for these advantages. Physical courage is an invaluable virtue, but we need not blind ourselves wholly to the future in order to possess it. Stability of mind and common sense cannot be too highly prized, but the possession of them does not make it impossible to see the things that do not yet exist. And it is this failure, above all others, that diminishes the pace of our social progress.

We must see them—these realities of the future: we must lift up our eyes. Ours is a democratic system and in its slow and cumbersome fashion it fulfils the wishes of common men and women. *They* must therefore see visions and dream dreams—not the deceptive illusions of Utopia but the next steps of the path in which we may safely walk. The man in the street must see a society that is strong and safe in the comfort of a wide association of states, a community in which no man is poor or unemployed, in which there is no servility to the pomp of wealth and of which children are the free and happy citizens. This society does not yet exist, but only because we do not see it—our eyes fixed upon the useful trifles of the world we know. There is nothing in this humble vision of a better social order that exceeds our physical or our intellectual power to create. We possess the military power to make ourselves safe, sufficient wealth to ensure that no one shall starve, the scientific understanding to tear the false gods from our hearts and to emancipate the child. We fail to secure these infinitely desirable ends because we do not see them—because our eyes are closed to the world that does not yet exist—the world we can have for the asking.

The greatest impediment to reaping the increasing benefits of science and the quiet heart is the profound conservatism of our people. No vested interest and no political minority could long stand in the way of the united and informed imagination of a free nation. We need only look upwards, peer more sharply through the forward mists of time, to walk into the light of a sunnier day.

A Better Society—Socialism and the British Tradition

I come to the last reason for the defence of our way of life. I believe that it contains, more certainly than any other, the means for its own improvement.

I believe most profoundly that we can remedy the evils to which I have called attention in the preceding pages: economic and social inequality, our vandalism and our unimaginativeness. We can extend the help that we give to one another until we have built, unwittingly, a better society.

The most fruitful central idea for our future is, I feel sure, to be found in the main doctrine of the British Labour Party.

I am a member of that Party and I believe that my Party has made, and will continue to make, an invaluable contribution to the political discussion that proceeds continuously within the nation and determines the development of our institutions. In particular, I feel convinced that the faith of the Party in a moderate and democratic form of Socialism is a natural outcome of our slowly growing faith in human liberty, equality and brotherhood and represents the next step in our social emancipation. Let me explain, briefly, what I mean.

The main evil from which we suffer and the main barrier to social progress is the disgraceful inequality in the distribution of income and property that we still tolerate.

We can only remove this evil by abolishing property as a main source of income for anyone. To do this, it will be necessary—as I previously argued—to modify the right of inheritance so that it is only possible to pass comparatively small sums of money or nothing at all from generation to generation. But this obvious truism leads to a further step in the argument. Property is the present method by which we direct our economic life. The owner of capital wealth controls —at least in legal theory [1]—the administration of industry; and if he is to do so no longer, then he must be replaced by some representative of the State. It is my personal conviction that this growth of social responsibility in the economic sphere —the coming into existence of a planned economy—will greatly improve the efficiency of our industry and finance in the long run. I believe that the substitution of conscious foresight for the instinctive adjustments of the competitive system, and the establishment of social authority in place of the search for private monopolistic control, will bring into existence a better balanced and a more securely progressive economy.

That is what I mean when I say that I am a Socialist. It is, however, necessary to add two further comments. In the *first* place it is important to emphasise that it is only necessary, and in the modern world it is only possible, to abolish property *as a main source of income*. The time has long gone past when it would be practicable or desirable to get rid of property altogether. Considerably more than half of the electorate now

---

[1] In point of fact the development of joint-stock enterprise and of the limited liability company has made the control of industry by its legal owners a fiction rather than a reality. Large companies are controlled by their Directors (who are only nominally responsible to the shareholders) and administered by their paid managers. The shareholder or *rentier* has become purely parasitic: deriving an income from a concern to which he contributes neither savings nor direction. For a further discussion of this subject see Berle and Means, *Modern Corporations*, or Chapter II of my *Politics of Democratic Socialism*.

possess a little stock of money—substantial and valuable to them—in a Post Office or Trustee Savings Bank, in a Friendly or Provident Society, in the "Co-op.". Property in this sense— i.e. *a small reserve* against a "rainy day"—has come to stay and is now so widely distributed among the population that it has become a means to personal liberty without creating social injustice. If everyone has a little property then no one gains an unfair advantage by the possession of it; while all enjoy a greater freedom. We should, therefore, as Socialists, seek to equalise the distribution of property rather than to liquidate it as an institution. It is too late, in any case, to do anything else. [1]

In the *second* place it is necessary to make plain that the social control (and ownership) of the larger basic industries does not imply, at least in my view, the desirability of setting up vast and cumbersome Government Departments to run each industry. In certain cases—the railways, electrical supply and the public utilities—a single unified plant and corresponding single administration is dictated by technical considerations. But the greater number of our industries (coalmining, textiles, shipbuilding, engineering, vehicles and the distributive trades) require a more divided and flexible arrangement. These commodities should be produced in a number of separate plants with a considerable degree of autonomy preserved for each of them—a de-centralisation of industrial management.

A socialised industry should be owned by the State and its technical management remain responsible to the nation. But it should retain all the advantages of small enterprise: plants that are small enough to be managed efficiently, enough of them to make a comparison between the competence of different managements enlightening, and a pricing and costing system useful. An efficiently planned economy must combine the advantages of unified direction and individual initiative. Like a modern Army or Navy, it should possess unity of command and the power to enforce the execution of a general strategy; but there must be independence, vitality and adaptability in the lower ranks of the administrative hierarchy and in the tactics of enterprise.

[1]For a further discussion of this point, see Chapter II of my *Politics of Democratic Socialism*.

This improvement in the efficiency of our economy and in the justice of our distributive arrangements is the beginning of a new social order. It will enable us to abolish unemployment and to extend the social services so that no member of our community need fall below a reasonable minimum of subsistence or live in daily fear of the desperate impoverishment that can still accompany unemployment or illness, old age or the sudden burden of family responsibilities. Moreover, substantial equality in the distribution of property will undermine the degrading differences of hierarchy and opportunity. We shall no longer be divided from one another by accents and education, by differences of economic interest and social class. We can then throw open the gates of knowledge and insist that every child shall receive the training of hand or eye or brain to which his inherited abilities suit him and see to it that the subsequent entry of young men and women into the occupations of lawyer and doctor, university teacher and industrial manager, becomes as easy as it now is difficult. By the same token the calling of the miner and the factory hand, the shop-girl and the railway porter will take on their full dignity: the equal in social honour of any useful service to the economy of a free society.

Economic equality will not only bring justice and social freedom but it will also release immense resources of ability now running to waste. No one can teach, as I have now done for ten years, both inside the walls of the universities and in the various types of extra-mural classes open to adult men and women (who have not taken a university degree), without knowing that we are failing to train a great number of first-class minds; while at the same moment we are allowing persons of third- and fourth-rate intelligence to crowd out our classes and waste our time merely because their parents possess enough money to pay the fees. This is social inefficiency of the worst type. And what is true of the particular natural talent that it is my professional business to train—academic or intellectual intelligence—must be true of all the other human gifts. We are neglecting immense, almost unimaginable, stores of vitality, imagination, executive ability, æsthetic and manual skill. All the ingenuity that we possess—all of which we should mobilise in our battle for happiness—could be brought to a rich harvest if we throw open the door of opportunity to our children.

The citadels of vandalism and the closed mind could then be forced. With knowledge would come power. Better educated men and women, freed from the bonds of social subservience, would see more clearly the society in which they wished to live and guide more firmly the conduct of democratic policy by which alone their hopes can slowly be established in the practice of the nation. Economic planning and social equality are the ideas upon whose slow growth the purification of our social order chiefly depends. [1]

This is, then, what I mean by a new or a better society. I believe we could create in one generation an economic system that provided continuous employment for every able-bodied worker; that maintained a steady and substantial rise in real wages; that would enable us to set a minimum standard of living, well above the present "poverty line", below which no single man, woman or child would be allowed to fall; in which all forms of education were open and free to the talented; in which property was equally distributed, thus becoming a growing source of personal freedom for us all. And upon the same foundation of this stable and progressive economy it would be possible to build a better society from which all educational inferiority had been removed; in which all men and women could live a richer life of friendship, free from the barriers of class distinction; that was able to protect the treasures of its ancient culture in town and country and could free the strong and merciful hand of science to cure physical and mental ill-health—holding back the dark waters of death to give us more life and lifting the burden of guilt and fear from the hearts of children in order that there may be more joy in the longer tale of our years.

This hope is *not* Utopian. It is a moderate and practicable programme of improvement. There is nothing in this list of changes that is not easily within our physical and intellectual powers to bring about. We need only become united in a wish

---

[1] I should of course argue (cf. *The Politics of Democratic Socialism*, Chapters I and IV) that the growth of these moderate and reasonable ideas itself depended upon the preservation and development of a certain type of *emotional* character in the individual and in the nation. But with these underlying determinants of character and behaviours I am not concerned in this book.

to possess this better order and in understanding that we can have it for the asking.

Let me repeat: there is nothing impossible in this vision. We have done far more difficult things and overcome greater barriers in the past. Lack of faith in the practicability of social progress—at least in this country—is only possible to those who obstinately concentrate their attention upon the great evils of this present time. A wider historical perspective—a single glance into the past—will reveal a wholly different story. Consider for a moment the last century of our social and economic development.

One hundred and one years ago—in 1841—Britain stood at the beginning of the "hungry forties". Let us suppose that a representative member of the toiling and starving industrial proletariat had been told, "In three generations your great-grandchildren will work for eight hours a day (instead of twelve) for an average real wage of three pounds a week (instead of twenty-five shillings); there will be universal adult suffrage (instead of a tiny electorate composed entirely of the rich), and universal and free elementary education (in place of your illiteracy); most of the unemployed will be supported by a state insurance and assistance scheme (instead of being humiliated, as you are, by the Poor Law); there will be regular provision for the sick and the aged (instead of the private charity and starvation from which you suffer); the sons of poor men will go to Oxford and Cambridge at the expense of the state and working men will enter the House of Commons in large numbers and occupy the highest offices in the state; the recognition of Trade Unions will be the rule, and not the exception; and most members of your class will possess a little property."

What would the poor man of 1841 have had to say to all that? He would, I suggest, have laughed bitterly. The prospect would have seemed preposterous to him—unrealisable in its optimism, a foolish dream. Sunk in poverty and ignorance, exhausted by endless hours of monotonous labour, burdened by an immense family, persecuted by the civil law against trade unions, patronised by the charity of the rich, tortured by the Poor Law, weakened throughout life by the horrible sanitary chaos of the early industrial slums and dying at an early age of curable diseases—the working man of 1841 would have been blind to the future—naturally but obstinately and obstructively blind.

So it is with us. Absorbed in the evils of our own time we do not see the great tide of social progress that sweeps slowly but inevitably through the affairs of free peoples. As we crouch in our shelters, wincing at the swish of the near bomb, we do not see the wider frame of time in which freedom brings, so deviously, a richer life. Nevertheless, the hand upon the face of the clock does move, though we cannot see it; and the poor people of London, crowded upon the wire mattresses in the Underground stations, seeking shelter from the ruthless savagery of Europe in 1941, are richer, healthier, more sane, freer and nearer the full dignity of humanity than their grand-fathers or their great-grandfathers, lying lost in the deeper and more hopeless miseries of the past.

The past justifies hope. So does the present. War is a fearful thing, destructive and bestial, but it does free men's minds. The only barriers to our swifter emancipation are the shackles of habitual thought and the darkness of the inward eye. War tears the familiar fabric of life to pieces, it kills and it tortures, but it breaks chains as well as homes and opens doors as well as graves. The physical destruction of London is a tragedy loaded with death and pain, but, bitter though it is, little as we wanted it, nevertheless we are now presented with the chance to rebuild a more spacious and beautiful city. In every field of our national life it is the same: the breakdown of our local government, the dislocation of our foreign trade, the immense re-ordering of our financial and industrial resources, the re-distribution of our population, the training of great armies and the overturning of favourite prejudices and fixed ideas, present us with an unwanted task, but with an astounding prospect of reconstruction—a wide-open doorway. Now is the time, when men's minds are free, to build our life anew.

Let us then embrace this unwelcome opportunity and gather an unexpected harvest from the blood-drenched field. Then the dead will not have died in vain.

But before we can gather harvests or walk through open doors, we must fight, endure and win this war. Victory is essential to social progress for two reasons.

The Case for Socialism

In the *first* place a continuity of our national freedom is a necessary condition for the healthy development of our society. If we lose this war we shall be governed by Germans; we shall become a subject race. Hitler will march in triumph through London. A German army of occupation will be maintained permanently at our expense, to command all the points of strategic importance for the domination of the island—Dover, Portsmouth, Plymouth, Bristol, Liverpool, Glasgow, the northern islands, Newcastle, York, Hull, Norwich and the Home Counties. We shall be ringed about with German steel and a sharp and burning dagger will be for ever directed at our hearts. A puppet government (headed by Sir Oswald Mosley?) or a German Gauleiter will be appointed to hold us in permanent subjection; and the German secret police will hunt down and destroy every centre of aristocratic, working class, or intellectual resistance. We shall be compelled to pay a regular and heavy contribution to the revenues of a vast and darkened German empire; and to salute German officers in our streets.

Under such conditions social progress would become impossible. We are a proud people, nurtured in freedom and power. We should devote all our energies to the dreadful tasks of underground resistance. We should give ourselves up to murder, striking down our tyrants by stealth, banding ourselves together in secret brotherhoods of blood and terror, becoming corroded with hatred, suffering in our own land the maddening degradation to which we condemned Ireland for three hundred years. This all seems fanciful now, but it would prove the sober and fearful logic of defeat.

Furthermore, in the *second* place, we must preserve our democratic form of government if our community is to secure a richer life for all its members. The revolutionary improvements that have taken place in the standard of life and the social freedom of our people during the last hundred years have been deeply influenced, and partly caused, by the pressure of common opinion. The mode of its operation has been obscure, devious, and peculiarly British. Public opinion in this country has never, until recent years, been particularly well informed on public policy; and it has never been consciously creative or revolutionary. Yet it has, in fact, been both. By the expression of discontent, by the rejection of unwanted change and the uncovering of secret abuses, by working the unimpressive machinery of meetings, leagues and parties, by inoffensive demonstrations and petitions and by the ballot box, it has slowly, imperceptibly, pressed into existence the society that it desired.

Without this incoherent activity the franchise would never have been extended, Trade Unions would not have been freed from the restrictions of an unfriendly law, primary education, old age pensions, unemployment and health insurance, and the emancipation of economic activity from the dead restrictions of the past, would never have been secured. The case for these reforms was normally crystallised and stated by enlightened minorities (often middle-class and intellectual), but Cobden and Shaftesbury and Gladstone, Peel, Lloyd George and Fisher would never have overcome the immense weight of political inertia and vested interest unless their call had been supported by the deeper sound of the public voice.

It is in this sense that we are fighting for democracy and "socialism". The victory of the blood-stained Hitler, of the efficient and frenzied German army, of the powerful and dark-minded German people, will rob us not only of freedom, democracy and the precious fruit of our established institutions but also of the slow perfection of a social progress which springs from the deep will of the people and is securely grounded in general acceptance.

The appearance of this better society—more just, more free, more happy than any we have yet known—will not come suddenly after the victory has been won.[1] The killing of millions of men, women and children, the destruction of whole cities and the sinking of a large part of the world's shipping, will not extend the reign of love and prosperity. It will only prevent the victory of hatred and oppression.

But that, in the long run, will be enough. We shall secure

---

[1] In this war we have not encouraged ourselves, I am glad to say, by the false hope that victory in it will solve all our internal and external problems. We do not delude ourselves by saying that this is "a war to end war" or "to build homes fit for heroes to live in". We recognise that we shall be faced by immense difficulties. Indeed this mood of disillusionment has gone too far and there is a danger that despair will paralyse the springs of action. One even hears people say: "It will be terrible *after* the war." This is, in my view, an absurd exaggeration. There is no reason why we should not solve all the problems with which we shall be faced so long as we exhibit reasonable foresight and determination.

another space, perhaps longer this time, in which to live freely. We shall resume the slow march of our great society. Men and women of learning and goodwill, drawn from all classes, will show us the way to cure unemployment, to achieve social equality, to make children happier; and once more the heavy tides of general opinion will surge uncertainly upwards, flooding secretly the forward channels of contentment.

We shall build this new society although we shall not even know that we are doing so. It will not be called socialism. It will not be called anything. The disgruntled minorities of extremists, whom we shall always have with us, will continue to deny that any improvement whatever has taken place. But a new society, beyond our present hopes, will surely come; and in one generation (in my lifetime if I survive for the normal span of years) we shall add inches to our physical height, extend the expectation of life, conquer unemployment, increase the standard of living by one-half; establish substantial equality of wealth and opportunity; cleanse our minds from a great weight of neurotic guilt and fear; becoming healthier, happier, richer, stronger, freer men and women—slowly attaining the certain dignity of our noble promise. This is a reasonable, a modest expectation. This is the reward of victory. We fight for the future as well as the past.

DEMOCRACY AND SOCIALISM
IN GREAT BRITAIN[1]

This article contains a review of two books—Mr. Bassett's "Essentials of Parliamentary Democracy" and Mr. Dalton's "Practical Socialism for Britain"—published in 1935. I have thought it worth reprinting for two reasons:

First, *the two books remain surprisingly fresh and contemporary in interest. Mr. Bassett's book is still the best analysis of, and statement of the case for British political practice. Mr. Dalton's is the only available account, before the event, of the domestic policy of a Labour Government. All the main problems of the relation between Socialism and democracy arise in the course of the review and most of the conclusions (including the criticisms) stand justified, at least in my view, by practical experience. In particular I should contend that the achievements of the Labour Government have shown that speed in legislation and administrative action is consistent with the maintenance of full political democracy and that accurate pricing and costing is essential to the efficiency of a planned economy.*

Secondly, *the review and Mr. Dalton's book serve to show that political prophecy, in general terms, is not impossible. It is amazing to see how much of what Mr. Dalton said could and should be done has, in fact, been accomplished.*

PRACTICAL political discussion in Britain to-day centres upon two questions. Can we prevent another European War? Can we transfer economic power to the state by purely democratic methods? These two books[2] constitute a major contribution to the elucidation of the second of the problems, and Dr. Dalton's work contains an important reference to the first.

Mr. Bassett's *Essentials of Parliamentary Democracy* is the best

---

[1] First published in the *Political Quarterly* for 1935.
[2] *The Essentials of Parliamentary Democracy*. R. Bassett. *Macmillan.* 7s. 6d. *Practical Socialism for Britain*. Hugh Dalton. *Routledge.* 5s.

contemporary discussion of the limitations and achievements of British democratic practice. It establishes by the most careful historical and reflective analysis the following propositions:

1 That the success of British Parliamentary institutions has not been dependent upon the uninterrupted existence of a "two-party system" (Chapters II and III). There is therefore no substance in the view that democracy must break down because the party groupings have become more complex.

2 Mr. Bassett then argues that democracy is not a state of society but a method of taking decisions about the state of society (Chapter IV). Democracy cannot be identified with social equality or personal freedom or their opposites, or indeed with any general condition of the social order whatever. Any form of society is compatible with the method of resolving differences within it by discussion, a search for agreement, mutual toleration, and freedom of political association. It is the method which is the true definition of democracy and the most fundamental thing in the political constitution of the state. The most important question which arises when powerful groups disagree is not what they disagree about, but whether or not they can agree as to the method by which their disagreement is to be resolved. Mr. Bassett unquestionably proves a confusion of mind—or at least of terminology—in those who use the term democracy to describe their private ideal of society and who fail to apprehend that the only "agreement about fundamentals" which is necessary is the agreement not to resort to force in the settlement of disputes.

3 Mr. Bassett is not content to define democracy. He proceeds to defend it in Chapters V and VI. He here constructs the best defence of political compromise in existence. Echoing the words of the Trimmer he shows that the principles of moderation and agreement are not due to the weakness of muddleheaded and nerveless politicians, but express the fundamental unity of the nation, and are the essential requirement of internal political peace. They are the embodiment of the sad lesson of history that unrestrained faction and civil war leave all questions unsettled and all parties, if not defeated, infinitely the poorer in spiritual achievement.

The book concludes with a brilliant and sustained attack on those sections of English political opinion which pay lip service to democracy—especially "true" democracy—but pour scorn upon the use of democratic methods and advocate policies that could only be carried into effect by a suspension of the orderly sequence of General Elections. Mr. Bassett demonstrates convincingly that such people, whether they confess it or not, are in favour of a dictatorship and the suppression of political liberty. For this section alone the book is of the utmost importance. In dealing with the honest dictatorship parties, Mr. Bassett emphasises the point (pp. 249–250) that such organisations—both Fascist and Communist—have no claim to the liberties they propose to destroy. Democrats are not required by their principles to hand over the reins of government to people who will beat them to death.

Mr. Bassett's book, as it stands, exhibits in my view a serious weakness in two respects. Firstly, it does not really meet, as it could do, the Class War analysis of political action on its own ground. Mr. Bassett does not state, as he might, the double refutation of this religion of the modern world. He does not point out with sufficient emphasis the falseness of supposing that beyond the level of subsistence human beings are purely economic agents or that the record of their action—the course of history—is a story of their economic struggles. Nor does he show that even if this were the case it would still be illogical to conclude that the road to complete political and social freedom must lie through the supersession of that form of liberty we have already achieved. I would recommend this fundamentally important and widely accepted political philosophy for the further exercise of Mr. Bassett's remarkable gifts of historical analysis and dialectical invective.

In the second place there are a number of unsatisfactory points in the treatment of political action. Mr. Bassett's assessment of political reality over-emphasises the rational. At least he under-estimates the importance of the irrational element in human affairs. This understatement appears in several parts of the book. Then there is a confusion over the problem of leadership in democracy. The gift of a leader is not, as Mr. Bassett suggests, to keep the extremist elements of his party in check, but to proceed in all matters—including the controversial ones—as rapidly as is compatible with preventing the revolt of the party's opponents in the long run. Mr. Bassett's whole treatment of "speed" in legislative and administrative action is a trifle disingenuous. He safeguards himself with all sorts of saving clauses—stipulating that political action may be swift when agreement is general—but the real weight of his argument supports the view that those of us who are true democrats must be prepared to pay a heavy price for liberty in the form of slow change. Nothing in my view could be more untrue or more dangerous for democracy. Mr. Bassett neglects in his treatment of Planning and the case for Socialism both the urgency of the problems and the great intricacy of economic legislation. He seems blind to the lamentable failure of the social will in England since the War. The tragedy has been and still is, not that minorities have been driven near to the point of rebellion by ruthless speed, but that numberless changes desired by the vast majority of the people have been successfully opposed by complacent minorities. Democracy cannot hope to survive in the modern world unless it can produce parties of determination and vision prepared to act rapidly on a wide legislative and administrative front without oppression and without cruelty. Act they must. Enthusiasm cannot be raised inside party organisations indefinitely and always frustrated with dilatoriness and futility.

The heart of the problem lies here. The difficulty of achieving democratic Socialism by peaceful means consists in devising a programme for the Labour Party which will fulfil three conditions:

1 It must, at the very least, include a transfer of a substantial increase of economic power to the Government, otherwise it will represent no real advance towards the establishment of a socialist democracy.

2 It must not provoke the opponents of Socialism to appeal to force or frighten them into an uncontrollable financial panic. In either case there would be a breakdown in the normal processes of peaceful government.

3 On the other hand it is equally essential that the programme of the Labour Party should retain the loyalty of a very large proportion of its followers. A strong and united party organisation is essential for the execution of a complex programme. Unless some platform can be found which will fulfil the last two conditions the possibility of a peaceful transition

to a social democracy has already gone. Neither the possibility of preserving democracy nor achieving Socialism has necessarily disappeared, but the establishment of the one by the other will be impossible. But if any programme can be discovered which will not drive the Opposition into armed revolt or the rank and file of the Labour Party into the arms of the Communists, the problem of the peaceful transition has been solved. For the transfer of economic power to the Government is the first condition, but in my own view the only condition, of ultimate success.

It is with this analysis in mind that the reader should turn to *Practical Socialism for Britain.* It is a unique book among recent publications. It is the only book in existence which contains a careful, sober and highly persuasive defence of the broad principles of the policy of the Labour Party as set forth in the official document, "For Socialism and Peace." The proposals for action defended by Dr. Dalton can be classified under four heads:

1 He proposes the very rapid reform of the machinery of legislation by the time-tabling of the Government's legislative programme for the whole of the session, the simplification of bills, and the freeing of certain days to enable the committee stage of several bills to be taken at once. In addition he proposes the election of a small salaried Second Chamber by a First Chamber and an age limit for Parliamentary candidates (of 65) and for Cabinet Ministers (of 70). The Second Chamber becomes a useful repository for wise but aged professional politicians. By those means the output of legislation could be greatly increased. (Part II.)

2 With the decks cleared for action in this way the Government should proceed to the socialisation of a number of basic industries—transport, power, coal, armaments, iron and steel, and a gradual acquisition of land (Part III)—and to the use of the power so obtained to control and direct industrial development, to raise investment in the basic industries, and to carry out geographical planning (Part V). Nationalisation is to be accompanied by "fair" compensation (Chapter XVIII) and associated with the representation of the workers on the Board of Control by ministerial selection after consultation with the Trade Unions (pp. 163–164).

3 Power over financial affairs is to be sought through the

nationalisation of the Bank of England (Chapter XXI), the control of the quantity (Chapter XXII) and direction (Chapter XXV) of long term investment through the machinery of a National Investment Board, but only of the Joint Stock Banks if they refuse to co-operate with the Government (p. 237).

4 The approach to equality is to be begun during the first period of office of the Labour Government, (*a*) in the early stages, by the extension of the social services in obvious ways as rapidly as a Budget balanced on Current Account will permit (Chapter XXV), and (*b*) in the later stages of the Government's life, by a most ingenious scheme of acquiring property at inheritance in exchange for terminable annuities (pp. 341–343).

It is impossible to do justice in a short review to the careful reasoning with which Dr. Dalton seeks to establish his conclusions. The discussions of Parliamentary Reform and geographical planning are masterpieces of clear exposition and persuasive argument. The proposals are limited, definite and practicable. The book, indeed, conveys in every chapter the sense of a mind acquainted with the detail of legislative and administrative action—aware of its possibilities and its limitations. In this respect it exhibits a sharp and welcome difference from the arm-chair legislative "plans" of which recent books on this subject have been full. It is the most responsible and therefore the most persuasive book on political programmes yet published.

I am not concerned so much with the detail of these proposals. No one will agree with all that Dr. Dalton suggests. Certainly I do not. [1] The more important question is whether

[1]In particular I disagree with Dr. Dalton on two important technical points: (*a*) I think that he greatly underestimates the significance of the Joint Stock Banks to a Socialist Government and of short term credit to an expansionist programme. Dr. Dalton says: (p. 231)

"In the execution of a Socialist financial policy the role of short term credits from the banks is less important than is sometimes supposed. It has been one of the faults of capitalist finance to rely too much on short term credit. Some of our basic industries and services, such as transport, have no need for short term credit at all. . . ."

This is scarcely the point. Banks are not wanted merely to transmit voluntary saving from the public to industry or to finance long term investment. Their active co-operation is required to prevent panics and to press up the volume of funds available for the transaction of monetary business. I cannot believe that a Socialist Government is safe from financial panic with the Bank of England alone. It must at least control the foreign exchange activities of the Joint Stock Banks. Nor do I see how the success of an expansionist programme can be guaranteed without a control of their liquidity and security policies. It is true that control is important a programme of this type offers a solution to the general problem of peaceful transition. Does it fulfil the three conditions laid down above? In my view there can be no question that it does.

It undoubtedly fulfils the first criterion. There will be a substantial transfer of economic power to the Government if half these proposals are carried through. There will even be a programme of purely equalitarian measures in the Government's first period of office. The programme is plainly a step towards socialism. It is also compatible with the second principle. This programme, though repugnant to the Right, could not press them to the point of armed revolt. The provision of compensation which is just between individuals and only expropriates future generations, makes certain of that. The programme may not avoid a financial panic, but a panic is the easiest thing in the world to control if the correct administrative steps are taken—as we have just seen in America. The only point of doubt lies in the third criterion. Will it retain the enthusiasm of the greater part of the Labour Party? It is not a spectacular programme. On the other hand the experiences of 1929–1931 so discouraged Utopian expectations in the party that I cannot help thinking that it will accept willingly any Government which begins with a vigorous attempt to transfer power to the state. If reasonable opinion is united within the party on a programme of determined but moderate socialisation, I believe that the Labour Party can be inspirited by it.

Will such a programme be implemented by the party? There is the rub. *Dr. Dalton's book makes it clear, once and for all, that the difficulty does not lie in programme building.* A suitable

---

while ownership is not. The real question at this point is not whether control is necessary but whether it can be obtained without ownership. Dr. Dalton does not disprove the necessity for ownership.

(*b*) Again in Chapter XXIV on "The Nature and Objects of Economic Planning," I believe that Dr. Dalton comes to the wrong conclusion about the significance of price theory in a Planned Economy. The theory of value constructed by economists has been used as an argument against Planning. Used in this way it is an important but invalid argument. But I do not see that Dr. Dalton establishes in the least that the guidance of prices is not of fundamental importance in securing an important kind of economic freedom. The freedom to obtain goods in the most preferred relation to each other is a freedom that should be denied to no person and no society. Why should it be? It is independent of the distribution of income and the size of income. It is more important to the poor than to the rich. What conceivable reason can there be on the grounds of democracy or socialism for destroying this liberty?

programme can be constructed. But has the party come to possess the intellectual equipment and the spiritual force to carry it through? Or is it also infected with the empty heart and shaken will which has characterised our national life since the dark days of war and during this restless "peace"?

These questions bring into high relief the historical failure of the Socialist League. There is nothing wrong with the Labour Party's *programme*. The only alternative to it is the use of a half-baked Marxian jargon and the elaboration of revolutionary proposals without the organisation of revolutionary force. That is a sickening intellectual spectacle. But there was a great opportunity—and perhaps there still is—for an independent socialist body to arm the party with intellectual penetration and emotional force behind a programme with which all serious democratic socialists can agree. Research and education—those were and still are the needs of the party. But that work has not been performed by the League. Instead it has frittered away its opportunity in the preparation of contrary programmes on home and foreign policy that can be riddled and sunk with intellectual criticism.

PROBLEMS OF A PLANNED ECONOMY

Paper III

THE IMPORTANCE OF PLANNING[1]

This brief Chapter contains my answer to three important questions:
(a) Why is centralised planning a superior form of economic organisation to that of free enterprise?
(b) How should authority be organised and distributed in a planned economy?
(c) What part should pricing and costing play in a planned economy?
Most of the answers I give are now, rightly or wrongly, commonly accepted by democratic socialist planners.

"WE ARE all Socialists now," said Sir William Harcourt in 1894. We are certainly not all Socialists in post-War Europe. The last few years have seen a whole-sale destruction of Socialist Parties on the continent and the election of an overwhelming anti-Socialist majority to the English House of Commons.

But it would be almost true to say that "we are all *Planners* now." The collapse of the popular faith in *laissez-faire* has proceeded with spectacular rapidity in this country and all over the world since the War. There now exists a completely planned economy in Russia, a bold and far-reaching attempt at general planning in America, an extension of the economic power of authoritarian governments in Italy and Germany, and the rudiments of financial and agricultural planning in England. Indeed, in this country planning has become one of the many subjects that scarcely enters into party controversy. The Labour Party proposes to socialise, and thereafter to plan a large sector of industry by the creation of ten or twelve public corporations. It is unquestionably a planning Party. But it was the Conservative Party which passed the Electrical Supply Act of 1928, placed the London Passenger Transport Bill on

[1]First appeared as a contribution to *New Trends in Socialism* (Chapter IX)—a book edited by Professor G. E. C. Catlin and published by Messrs. Lovat Dickson in 1935.

the Statute Book, set up the Exchange Equalisation Fund, has cartelised sections of the agricultural industry, is making some attempt to re-organise and unify the iron and steel industry, is subsidising shipping and proposes to begin the first stages of geographical planning. All these measures involve in greater or less degree the social control of industry. There is therefore an important agreement between the largest parties in the State on the supersession of private enterprise in the guidance of economic affairs.

There is, however, no such general agreement about the ends which the growing power of the Central Government shall be made to serve. The Conservative Party is not hypocritical in its opposition to the Labour Party, since it is radically opposed to the reform of society which the Labour Party intends. It is *Socialism*, and not economic planning that is in dispute. These two things are often confused, but they are in fact quite different, and it is of the greatest importance to understand their true relations. In particular it is necessary in this article to consider the importance of planning both to Socialists and to anti-Socialists.

Before this can be done we must define the meaning of economic planning with some precision. The term is used in current speech to describe widely different types of economic reform. It is applied indiscriminately to large-scale and fundamental changes in economic institutions, such as those carried through in the Russian economy, and to the comparatively small alterations which the cartelisation of the English milk industry involves. It is necessary to distinguish between:

(*a*) Planning, meaning simply the *intervention of the Government in a particular industry* at a time when the greater part of the economy still remains in private hands, and

(*b*) Planning which results in the *general supersession of individual enterprise* as the source of economic decisions.

This distinction is of importance, because the basis of authority and the probable results of the two types of planning are quite different. It is, for example, quite untrue, as certain opponents of Planning always argue, that *general* planning will be no more than the sum of a large number of interferences with a private enterprise economy. It would be just as sensible to argue that civilisation is nothing more than the destruction

42

of primitive culture. The substitution of one set of institutions for another, whether better or worse, is quite different from the arbitrary frustration of existing arrangements. Thus, while it is easy for certain economists to prove that planning of the first type will result in nothing more than the interference with adjustments to the real situation which would be made by private enterprise and will lead to the use of the new powers created by unification to restrict output and hold up prices, it does not follow that the same thing will be true when central control is generalised and private interest is replaced over a large field of industrial activity.[1] To begin with, in the case of general planning, the source of authority is no longer an industrial corporation, but an *inter-industrial* body. This makes the pull of conflicting interests more apparent and the implication of alternative courses more plain. There is, for example, no evidence that the Russian economy, whatever its other economic shortcomings, has been characterised by any attempt to restrict production. Social interests are necessarily more strongly represented in the machinery of generalised planning than in particular interferences, and it is confusing to call these two types of economic change by the same name.

It is also necessary to be clear about two different uses to which the machinery of centralised control may be put. Planning does not in the least imply the existence of *a* Plan—in the sense of an arbitrary industrial budget which lays down in advance the volume of output for different industries. Planning does not, and should not, imply any dogmatism about the future. It is not possible to tell in detail what will happen to human tastes, to technical invention, to general standards of security and well-being. It would therefore be foolish in the extreme to attempt to lay down plans which could not be amended quickly in the light of changing social requirements. There is no power yet known to man whereby he can foretell the movements of human society with the precision and degree of certainty that is exhibited by the physical sciences. There is as yet no economic astronomer, and until this gentleman has made his appearance there can be no reasonable rigidity or permanence in the absolute and relative outputs of the various industrial products.

[1]Cf. Robbins, *The Great Depression*, Chapter VIII.

Problems of Economic Planning

What, then, is the true characteristic of Planning? If it does not involve the construction of a single plan, and is nevertheless something more than the cartelisation of particular industries, what is the correct definition of its essential nature? The element common to all the forms of new control we regard as "Planning" is the extension of the size of the unit of management and the consequent enlargement of the field surveyed when any economic decision is taken. The diagnostic property of an unplanned economy is the requirement that all decisions should be taken by individual supervisors in only a small—indeed, an infinitesimal—area of the industrial world. Under conditions of perfect competition—the pure type of the unplanned economy—the individual producer controls so small a part of the total output of a single commodity that he can exert no influence upon the price of anything that he either buys or sells. His field of vision is restricted to the technical organisation of his own factory or workshop, and no individual or corporation possesses any power to control the prices or output of the industry. All forms of planning machinery extend the area of economic life surveyed by the deciding authority and increase the number and importance of the economic quantities that can be controlled by some one.

The extension of control can take place in two stages. There is first the grouping of production units making the same or closely related products into one corporation. This is the case of the cartelisation, incorporation or socialisation of a single industry. Electrical production and London passenger transport are English examples of this type. The second and more important extension is that which brings a group of industries and economic activities, and in the limit the whole economic field, under the survey and control of a single authority—termed the Supreme Economic Authority. This would be the result of the present proposals of the English Labour Party, and is the ideal towards which the Roosevelt Administration in America is at present struggling. It is this extension of the area of survey and control which is the definitive thing about all forms of Planning.

2 What is the importance of Planning so defined in the first place to Socialists and in the second place to those who are interested in economic efficiency? Socialists may be described

44

as those who believe it to be of ethical and practical importance to remove inequality between persons and classes in so far as it is based upon the inheritance of property and the institutions created for the service of the rich. To people who hold such views the setting up and subsequently the successful operation of a certain form of Planning is of the first importance.

Now, there is nothing in my definition of Planning to say who is to plan and to what end. It is, however, perfectly clear that social equality cannot be achieved in an unplanned economy. The capitalist system depends for its power of adjustment upon the search for the reward distributed to private property in the means of production and for its power to grow upon the savings derived from large private incomes. It is therefore apparent that any sustained attempt to impair the operations of the profit motive and to destroy inequality in the distribution of wealth, without providing an alternative method of accumulating capital, will lead to a breakdown. The time will come when either the scheme of transferring income must be stopped or the capitalist system will cease to function. Such a disastrous alternative must at all costs be prevented, and it can only be done by removing the power to make economic decisions from the hands of property-owners. They must be vested in the State or the representatives of the State.

To a Socialist the mere change in the seat of power is not sufficient. It is a means to an end. The end consists in the creation of a society in which men are both free and equal. But, while the institution of some form of Planning is not the object, it is the indispensable preliminary means for the attainment of the new society. It is indispensable for the reasons just stated. It is preliminary because men must live and work during the period of social change—a period which may be long and difficult. To a Socialist, therefore, the setting up of a comprehensive machinery for the control of the means of production is of the most urgent importance.

3. But, as we have seen it is not only Socialists who are interested in Planning—not only Socialists who believe in it. An increasing number of thinking men and women are coming to the conclusion that centralised control is a better method of organising production, apart altogether from the kind of social

superstructure subsequently created within it. They believe that Planning is an essentially more *efficient* method of organising economic life.

The matter is, of course, also of the greatest importance for Socialists. If Socialism is to be obtained by democratic methods, it is necessary that, as a system, it should work efficiently from the earliest possible moment—and "work efficiently" in a sense that the ordinary elector can appreciate. Without in the least taking the cynical view that the ordinary elector is indifferent to questions of status and social freedom, it would be flying in the face of plain reality to deny that "the man in the street" judges the economic efficiency of any system by the degree of security in employment and the level of real wages it brings to him. To him Planning will "work" if it brings about a sustained rise in employment and a noticeable increase in the general standard of living. The first stages of Socialism—by which I mean the first period of five years in which a Labour Government seeks to transfer a large sector of industry to social ownership—will be judged by the extent to which "prosperity" is restored during the lifetime of that Government. Any Socialist, therefore, who wishes to secure for the next Labour Government the second period of office necessary for a further advance to social change, and who does not propose to obtain that extended period by unconstitutional and revolutionary methods, will be deeply concerned with the power of Planning to increase the means of livelihood and consumption.

We must therefore examine the efficiency of Planning as a method of directing economic life.

There are three charges which have been brought against Planning—both by professional economists and by business men. It has been argued that a Planned Economy will be a muddled economy because it will lack the automatic guide to productive activity provided by a pricing system; [1] that it will lack the necessary incentives to secure efficient management; and that it will be unable to make adequate provision for the future. [2] These are serious charges and must be considered.

The first of them—that Planning will lead to chaos because

---

[1] See *Collectivist Economic Planning*, III, Mises: "Economic Calculus in the Socialist Commonwealth," and F. von Hayek: "The Present State of the Debate."
[2] Professor Robbins, *The Great Depression*, Chap. VII, §§ 6–8; Chap. IX, § 3.

it lacks the automatic guidance of prices—can be advanced in two forms. It may either be said that a Planned Economy *cannot* have a pricing system because the institutions of central control render accurate prices impossible, or that although prices can exist their guidance *will not*, in fact, be followed by a Planning Authority. These two versions of the argument are radically different. The first assumes that there is some logical contradiction between prices and central control, while the second argument must be based upon social and psychological assumptions. It could only be justified by a demonstration that people will necessarily be foolish and pigheaded in a society which has chosen to control its economic life. It is of the greatest interest to notice that the arguments of *laissez-faire* economists have recently shifted their emphasis sharply from the one trend of argument to the other. [1] This is so for three reasons:

(*a*) In the first place, Russia, a centrally Planned economy, is plainly operating a price system of a sort. The Communist Party attempted in the first instance to abandon economic calculus altogether, and the result was unspeakably disastrous. [2] The present Russian system including the Five-Year Plan is therefore one which is based fundamentally upon prices. The Plan or industrial budget is a schedule of total prices; industries are rationed in the monetary funds placed at their disposal; costs are calculated; and prices are charged for finished products at every stage. No one is saying that their price system is accurate or that relative prices are made the sole criterion of productive policy. But that a price system can exist side by side with the central control of production is demonstrated beyond the possibility of refutation by Russian economic history.

(*b*) And, in the second place, it cannot be denied that any price system, however crude, must result in *some* kind of rational

---

[1] It is, for instance, perfectly obvious that this is the case, if *Collectivist Economic Planning* is examined carefully. It will be found that, whereas Professor Mises, in the earlier article "Economic Calculus in the Socialist Commonwealth," simply takes it as axiomatic that a Collectivist economy must dispense with prices, and regards it as his business to prove that it will therefore get into a muddle, Professor Hayek in his later article simply tries to prove that an *accurate* pricing system is out of the question. To do this he has finally to fall back to the second line of argument, that although the Planning Authority could "play" at competition (*sic*), it would never, in fact, dispose its resources in the indicated ways.

[2] See Dobb's *Russian Economic Development: War Communism*, and Mrs. Wootton's *Plan or No Plan*, Chap. II, § 2.

guidance as long as consumers are left free to spend their money as they please and a rough uniformity of costing practice is enforced upon all industries at once. Economists are perfectly right to insist that only the most delicate assessment of the value of economic resources in alternative uses will secure a *perfect* adaptation of production to the needs of society. But the degree of adaptation can vary very greatly, and any Planning Authority which insists upon a uniform assessment of values and costs will be able to make correspondingly wide adjustments to changing tastes and changing conditions. Even in the Russian price system where no payment is made for land or for the differences of individual efficiency within large groups of workers, it is obvious that the Central Authority could detect large divergences between the value produced and the cost incurred in any particular line of production by the tendency for stocks to change or prices to move at any given level of output. And this reasoning applies to every type of product. Crude price systems mean crude adjustment. Delicate price systems mean delicate adjustment. But it is only the absence of any price system which means no adjustment.

(*c*) From these two lines of investigation it must follow that there is no formal or logical contradiction between planning and pricing. It is perfectly possible for a centralised authority to order a price system to appear and to follow the guidance it necessarily gives. *There is no necessary connection between the form of the authority by which decisions are taken and the principles according to which the decisions are made.* It would be just as sensible to argue that the organisation of the medical profession under a National Council which laid down rules of professional conduct made it impossible to practise sound medicine as to affirm that the creation of a governing body for industry made it *impossible* to take wise economic decisions. It all depends upon what the Central Authority chooses to do.

Consequently the emphasis of the attack upon Planning has, in recent years, shifted back to the second charge, that, despite the logical possibility of pricing and wise planning, such wisdom will not in fact be exhibited by central authorities. I know of no reasoned defence of the view that central control will strengthen social unreason, but the two specific charges that proper incentive will be lacking and that socialist planning will be incapable of capital accumulation have been made and must be met.

The first of these charges can scarcely be sustained after the experience of authoritarian industrial management witnessed in Europe during and after the War. The sanctions against mismanagement provided by capitalism are bankruptcy and unemployment. The incentive for rapid and socially desirable activity is the hope of larger real incomes. There is no conceivable reason why a Central Authority should not impose just as strong, and even stronger, negative checks and provide the same type of positive inducement. Indeed, the experience of Planned Economies suggests that the danger with respect to negative checks is that they will be made too severe rather than too mild. The firing squad and the swamps of Siberia have featured too prominently as a reward for incompetent management in Russia, for example. And in the same way there is no reason in the nature of planning, and no great probability in practice, that differences in earnings will cease to be attached to grades of labour and skill which it is in the interests of society to develop and extend.

The only charge against Planning in which there remains the least shadow of substance is that a democratic and Socialist form of planning will find it difficult to secure funds for capital accumulation. It is obvious that the *authoritarian* economy in Russia has been guilty of *over*-saving rather than under-saving, but in this case it was possible to enforce the relative restriction of consumption by the bayonet and machine-gun. Would it be possible to do the same under a democratic régime in which Trade Union influence was strong?

It would be silly to deny that in a Socialist economy the pressure to raise wages in all industries at once would be sustained and grave. Nevertheless, if the natural desire on the part of each group of workers to increase the volume of their consumption is acceded to indefinitely, the rise in wages will eat into and finally altogether destroy the funds out of which the services of the Central Government and the building of new capital can alone be financed. The surplus arising in socialised industries must be owned by society and not by the group of workers in each industry. It must be administered by the Supreme Economic Authority for the good of the whole economy, and not absorbed by the increase in the standard of living of small groups. Otherwise economic progress will cease. To this point we shall return in discussing the conditions of efficient Planning.

4 An investigation of the case against Planning leaves us, then, with the conclusion that, while there is no ground for supposing that it is impossible for a centrally controlled system to be as wisely guided as an unplanned system, there is one obvious danger from which a democratically controlled Socialist economy may suffer and must be saved. But we must go on to ask if there are any reasons for supposing that a Planned Economy will be *more* efficient than an unplanned? [1] There are, in my view, at least four reasons for supposing that this will be the case:

(*a*) To begin with, a centrally controlled economy will be an economy with *open eyes*. It is the essence of an unplanned and competitive arrangement of industry that the persons who take decisions about output and investment should be blind. They control such a small fraction of the output of a single commodity, [2] and, therefore, take into account such a small part of the industrial field, that they are not and cannot be aware of the consequences of their own actions. They are not aware of the economic results. They do not even consider social repercussions. Competitive producers, for example, will tend to instal machinery with a view to increasing output without realising that all their fellow producers will be doing the same thing and that prices will be forced down in consequence. They will, in fact, be forced below the price which would justify the increased output. Moreover, they will throw labour out of employment without any regard to the results of such a step. Since as producers they are not forced to maintain their erstwhile employees until they—the employees—have found new

---

[1] It might at first sight seem absurd to set up a Planned Economy and then impose upon it the same principles of arrangement as obtined in a competitive order. Why, it might be asked, bother to set up Planning machinery if you only want to arrange resources in the same way as they will be arranged under competition? This argument is quite beside the point. In the first place, it is possible to set up a wholly different distributive and social system upon the basis of a Planned Economy, and, in the second place, there are the reasons given in the text for supposing that Planning will be a more efficient method of obtaining any set of ends whatever.

[2] At least, if they do not, they become monopolists, and the whole defence of Capitalism along these lines breaks down.

work, no final assessment of the cost of labour displacement is made by the private employer. Nevertheless, *society* has to bear the cost of maintaining the unemployed. Moreover, the sufferings of the displaced individuals as persons are part of the true cost to humanity of the technical change. In this and a thousand other ways the decisions taken in an unplanned economy must be shortsighted, irrational, self-frustrating and socially disastrous. There is no space to describe in detail the prejudice in favour of change, the wastage of human skill, and the continuous maladjustment which competitive industry exhibits under slowly changing conditions.[1]

All these limitations of vision and calculation could be swept away by central control. The consequences of every decision can be estimated however remote from the point of disturbance they may arise. Some allowance for it can then be made. When it is decided to instal an electrical drill in a coal mine it will be possible to take into account not only the immediate effect upon the cost of extracting coal, but also the influence upon market price of an all-round rise in the output of the mines, the opportunities for the re-employment of displaced coal hewers elsewhere, the costs of maintaining them during the transitional period, and even some allowance can be made for the loss of skill and happiness—a loss that can be brought to no direct pecuniary assessment. A central authority, because it is central—because that is to say it can survey the whole industrial field—can see things no individual producer can ever see and give weight to considerations that cannot play any part in the calculations of men engaged in competing with one another. The general officers on the hill must be able to see more than the ensign in the line of battle.

(*b*) Just as there is an extension of the field of cognition over the breadth of industry, so also is there an increase in the length of foresight in time. A Central Authority can take account of processes which are occurring so slowly, or will begin to occur so far in the future, that no single producer could be aware of their existence.

A Central Authority could have foreseen the long agony of

---

[1]A very good example of this is the continuous failure during a hundred years of an unplanned world agriculture to adapt itself to its slowly diminishing relative importance.

the hand-loom weavers at the beginning of the last century in this country, the slow and cruel pressure upon world agriculture of more recent times, the need for a large-scale redistribution of labour in England in the twenties of this century; and could have made adjustments on a sufficient scale and over a long enough period to prevent much of the suffering and disharmony that have scarred our economic and social life.

A Central Authority can foresee the exhaustion of raw materials, the wastage of natural resources of beauty and health, and the destruction of human life which the blind scrambling of short-period plans continuously ignores. Such an Authority would, if it were in existence, foresee in our own country the tragic waste of the countryside indiscriminate building is everywhere occasioning, discern the disastrous social and economic consequences of the continual movement of industry into the south, and tackle in its greater wisdom the task of assessing the real social requirements in respect of the geographical distribution of industry and employment.[1]

(*c*) One of the most important matters with which a Planning Authority will have to deal is the relation between finance and production. In no other field has the unplanned economy been less successful. The constant recurrence of depression and the instability of prosperity is one of the most marked features of capitalist society, and there is a virtual unanimity among economists that the wide movements of industrial activity are traceable to the mismanagement of the relation between credit policy and production. Moreover, the whole trend of recent thought on this subject has gone to show that, if it were possible to control one critical relation, the problem would be solved. The crucial relation is that between the savings of the public —the amount of money income which is not spent on consumption—and the money which is invested in setting up new capital. In an unplanned economy there are two sources of disequilibrium: (i) in the first place, the people who save and the people who invest are in no direct connection with each

[1]*Laissez-faire* economists sometimes argue that the correct distribution will be made by the process of costing up the various sites for the location of factories. This might be the case if it were not for the fact that all sorts of vitally important economic considerations—the health of the neighbourhood, the costs of transferring labour, the natural amenities which are destroyed, and the social capital in other areas which is wasted—find no place in the costings of an unplanned economy. Only a centralized control could assess the importance of these factors.

other, and it is no one's business to see that acts of saving are followed immediately by equal acts of investment; (ii) in the second place, private banking institutions are in a position to vary the volume of investment without any reference to the course of saving. These are two sources of serious instability and are responsible between them for a very considerable proportion of the unemployment which has afflicted Capitalism throughout its history. No doubt there are purely scientific problems of great intricacy which must be resolved before we can hope to create and maintain stable prosperity. In my view, a large proportion of this necessary preliminary scientific work has been brought to a successful conclusion in recent years. But, whether that is the case or not, it is quite certain that whatever the correct monetary policy may be, it can only be enforced upon private corporations by the creation of an Authority in the financial sphere with adequate powers to over-ride all private considerations in the interest of general harmony. It is therefore safe to say that cyclical oscillation—the major cause of unemployment—will never be cured without the creation of the institutions of centralised *monetary* control. The financial field provides one of the most important opportunities for a Planned Economy to prove more efficient than an unplanned.[1]

(*d*) Finally, there is one way in which a Socialist Economy may expect an increase in the volume and efficiency of the factors of production which is not available for any other sort of economy whatever—and that is in the attitude of the Trade Union worker to production. In an industrial world dominated by the struggle between organised property and organised labour for status and wealth, it is inevitable that all sorts of obstructive regulations should arise and "ca' canny" practices be enforced. These are, no doubt, partly due to the continuously recurring contractions in the demand for labour. But this is not wholly the case. A residuum of such resistance is wholly attributable to the dislike of the employer and the rights of property as such. There is, therefore, every reason to believe that there will be an increased willingness to relax such restrictions and to co-operate more willingly with the management side of industry when a Socialist Authority has raised the status of workers' representation and can provide full

[1]See Durbin, *The Problem of Credit Policy*, Chapter VIII.

employment for the working population. No doubt too much has been made of this "change of spirit" in the Socialist apologetics of the past. The probability of conflicts between the interests of workers organised in industrial groups and the general service of society is very real. But to assert that the socialisation of the means of production and distribution would release *no* new stores of vital productive energy in the labour force, would be to ignore the width and intensity of the Socialist sentiment which consciously or unconsciously animates the whole proletariat of a modern society.

5 If the arguments of this article are correct, it follows that, while there are no inherent and insuperable obstacles to prevent a centrally controlled economy from making wise distribution of the resources at its disposal, there are several reasons why it *could*, if it chose, make a better distribution and secure a greater volume of production. Will it do so? The answer to that question rests with the future and is not subject to rigid prophecy. A Socialist Planning Authority will probably make use of some of these opportunities and not of others. But it is possible to lay down with some degree of certainty the conditions for the successful operation of a planned system in Great Britain.

In the *first* place, it will be essential to set up some kind of Central Authority with power over industry and finance. And this for two reasons:

(*a*) It will not do merely to create a large number of powerful but autonomous Public Corporations. This is only Planning of the first degree. It is subject to manifold dangers and limitations. It is quite true that Public Corporations operating with legally limited rates of profits will not be able to exert the same kind of monopoly pressure as a purely private body placed in the same dominating position. But it will possess the power and the motive to restrict the volume of service rendered, and to raise prices or fail to lower them, in the interests of the workers and the management in that industry. If such dangerous syndicalist tendencies are to be overruled, some authority with power to fix prices, output, and investment must be set over the Public Corporations.

(*b*) Of even greater importance, since restriction is always the child of financial stringency, is the need to control the financial mechanisms of the economy. It is of supreme urgency, if the Planned Economy is to be rendered popular and therefore stable in the midst of a democracy, to see that the early days of central control are followed by an expansion of employment and a stabilisation at the higher level. This can only be done by control of banking and investment policy. The creation of a National Investment Board, the control of policy of the Joint Stock Banks and the use of the powers so acquired for the execution of a concerted plan of expansion and subsequent stabilisation are, in my view, a *sine qua non* condition of successful Planning. [1]

If this is the case, the process of socialisation must begin rather than end with the creation of a Supreme Economic Authority. It does not matter whether the Authority consists of a Planning Department with a responsible Minister at the head of it, or a sub-committee of the Cabinet with the responsible Minister in the Chair, or even a number of Commissioners under general Parliamentary control, as long as the body is not too big or cumbersome and is of a representative character. But it is of vital importance that one small body should have before it the relations between industry and industry on the one hand and industry and finance on the other. Only by this device is it reasonable to hope that the full advantages of central control can be secured.

In the *second* place, it is of great importance that an Authority with general powers should proceed upon the basis of a reasonable pricing and costing policy. Economists have been right to insist that the problem of distributing scarce resources between alternative employments exists for all economies—for a Socialist economy as much as a Capitalist. It is imperative to know what particular commodities are worth and how much they cost if any solution to the problem is to be found. As we have seen, it is not absolutely essential that the principles of costing should be accurate in every particular. They are certainly anything but accurate in existing competitive economies. The principles of costing under Socialist Planning will be less accurate in some important respects and more

---

[1]For a slightly fuller account of such a policy see Part II of my *Socialist Credit Policy* (Gollancz and New Fabian Research Bureau) and *The Problem of Credit Policy*, Chapter VII.

accurate in others. It will tend, for example, to obliterate the differences between the productivity of individuals within large groups of workers, but it will certainly assess to each type of production the general social disadvantages which private producers can shift on to the community. There is no reason why Socialist costing should not be as accurate as or even more accurate on balance than competitive costing—but costing there must be. If the Central Authority insists upon pricing outputs fairly, and secures uniform costing principles throughout the sector of socialised industry, the last requirement of efficiency—that of securing the distribution of labour and capital according to the differences between prices and costs—will arise. We can see the nature of this last requirement in the light of the general conclusion to which we are brought.

It has been the purpose of this article to emphasise that the importance of Planning to a democratic Socialist is twofold. In the first place, a transference of industry to social control is the pre-requisite political condition for any stable advance to a more just society. In the second place, Planning is vitally important in order to establish a more efficient economic system. This will render the approach to equality popular and, in any case, it is desirable for its own sake. In the establishment of a more efficient economy the most important single change lies undoubtedly in the cure of periodical depressions. But beyond that task, stretching out into the future when full employment is secured, there remains the double task of maintaining economic advance through the accumulation of capital and retaining the flexibility in the arrangement of the factors of production. Now, neither of these tasks can possibly be performed unless there is a willingness on the part of organised labour to adjust itself to the new conditions of national control. As we have already seen, the only way in which the accumulation of capital can be financed is by the withdrawal of part of the funds earned by socialised industries from the workers employed in them to finance the capital items in the industrial budget. Surpluses arising in socialised industries must not belong to the workers in such industries. They must belong to the State. And in the same way, if correct adjustments are to be made within the industrial structure, the vested interests of the workers in any particular industry must never be allowed to prevent contraction of employment if it is making losses or expansion if it is making profits. No one with a knowledge of Trade Union opinions and practices will doubt that this is one of the real problems of Socialist Planning.

The third, and perhaps the most important, requirement of efficient Planning is therefore the supersession in the Trade Union and Labour Movement in practice as well as in theory of the last elements of Syndicalism. All partial groups of workers by hand and brain—lawyers as well as bricklayers, postmen as well as doctors—must be prepared in the last resort to allow their own interests to be subordinated to the interests of the workers as a whole. It is scarcely necessary to point out that this does not mean that no regard is to be paid to the general human desire for stability and security. Nor does it mean that the vast majority of workers will not benefit by the processes of mutual concession that are demanded from us all. On the contrary, a rapid rate of capital accumulation and a reasonable degree of flexibility are of vital importance for the welfare of every single worker in his nature as a consumer. Only within these conditions can any individual enjoy a rapidly rising standard of living. The interests of all persons as consumers may be in conflict with the interests of particular groups of persons as producers. What is requisite for efficiency is that the interests of all should be served by a continuous process of concession on the part of particular groups. We must all mitigate our claims in order that others may mitigate their claims against us and that by compromise we may all live.

. The efficiency of Planning depends in the last resort upon the breadth and consistency of the Socialist faith which animates us. The organised workers who claim with justice that the interests of the community should not be over-ridden for the profits of the few should go on to add that those same interests must not be overridden for the wages of a few. The interests of the whole are sovereign over the interests of the part. In society we are born; by society we must live. To the centralised control of a democratic community our livelihood and our security must be submitted. It is the business of society to secure the welfare of all. To do so it must be able to set limits to the welfare of each one of us.

Paper IV

THE PROBLEMS OF THE
SOCIALISED SECTOR

The following Paper has not been published before. It was written in 1946. It serves to bring up to date my views on:

(a) the application of pricing and costing to the socialised sector of a planned economy.

(b) the necessity for decentralised administration within a socialised industry.

The first section of the article attempts to clear up the common confusion over efficiency that is compatible with economic planning and social equality.

Introduction

THE British economic system is, as usual, in a state of transition. It is moving from one principle of organisation (that of private enterprise) to another (that of social ownership and centralised direction).

This movement is not new. It began with the First World War, and it was sharply stimulated by the Great Depression of 1929–1932, by the Second World War, and by the coming to independent power, for the first time in our history, of a Socialist Party in the General Election of 1945.

I am not here concerned with the causes of this change in the direction of our development but with its consequences. Nor have I anything to say about the arguments for the creation of a planned economy, although I wholeheartedly believe in them. They are, however, very familiar by now, and as we are clearly committed to an experiment in socialism, it seems better to use the space at my disposal to raise some of the *problems* that consequently arise. [1]

The most obvious of these is the division of our economic

[1] Those still interested in the arguments for a planned economy may care to look at Douglas Jay's *The Socialist Case* and my article in the *Economic Journal* of 1936.

The Problems of the Socialised Sector

system into two parts—the expanding *socialised sector* in which the capital is owned by the State, and the contracting *private sector* in which the capital is still owned by individuals and companies and in which the directors and managers are responsible (in theory) to groups of shareholders.

The slowness of the change-over is clearly demonstrated by the probable relative size of these two parts of the system at the end of this Parliament. If the present Government is able to execute its electoral mandate without serious hindrance from the House of Lords, the following industries and services will have been taken over by 1949: The Bank of England, the Coal industry, Electricity and Gas, the Railways and a substantial part of Road Transport, Iron and Steel, Civil Aviation, Cables and Wireless. Speaking very roughly these industries and services at present employ 2 million persons—or just 20 per cent of the industrial population. If we add to that figure the 2 million employed directly by Central and Local Government and the 1.2 million who are still in the Armed Services, we arrive at a grand total of 5.2 million in the service of the State —out of the 21 million persons now seeking work.[1]

Hence the socialised sector, however widely defined, will only include 25 per cent of our human resources, while the private sector will continue to employ 75 per cent of all labour and 80 per cent of industrial labour.

The pace of change is, therefore, modest—as might be expected in this slow-moving country.

At the same time it is important to notice that the power of the State to direct our economic and industrial life is not limited by the extent of the socialised sector. The Government, while rapidly scrapping the right to control labour, has retained a large number of the powers taken during the war to influence the use of property. It looks at the moment (July 1946) as though we shall retain, for many years:

the power to control *prices;*
the power to control *borrowing* above a limit of £10,000;
the power to control *imports* of raw materials and foodstuffs;
the power to control *building* through a system of licences.

These rights, combined with the ancient prerogatives of taxation, borrowing and the making of grants, place an immense

[1]Central Statistical Office Monthly Digest of Statistics, May 1946.

accumulation of economic power in the hands of the Government. We stand committed, for good or ill, to the principle of centralised direction in our economic life.

Two very general points are worth mentioning, in passing. In the first place the growing economic power of the State is subject to one important limitation. Apart from conscription to the Armed Forces, and a rapidly diminishing use of the Essential Work Orders, the Government now has no right to dictate the distribution of labour, or to order any man or woman to take up, or remain in, any particular job. As citizens and producers we must be persuaded and cajoled into occupations of our own choice, since we cannot any longer be directed into them. This is as it should be since the right to choose one's job is a fundamental civil liberty to most Britons and central direction is only to be welcomed if it increases our personal freedom.

It is further important to realise that a growth in the economic power of the State need not compromise our political liberty since it rests in the hands of a democratically elected Parliament, and the guarantee of our freedoms remains where it always did, in the *political* constitution and practice of our society. Democracy is a method of making laws, anarchy an absence of law. And the extension of the rule of law in economic affairs is no exception to this generalisation. Anarchy is not freedom; nor is anarchic enterprise the necessary source of general liberty, either economic or political.

Before this brief digression we had seen that the combination of a growing socialised sector with general powers over prices, borrowing, importing, building, taxing and subsidies presents to the Government a formidable set of powers and responsibilities.

What arrangements have been made to exercise these powers and shoulder these responsibilities?

An administrative machine—corresponding to the Supreme Economic Authorities of more fully planned economies—has, in fact, been set up. This organisation has developed naturally out of that built up during the war, and was explained to the country by Mr. Winston Churchill (then Prime Minister) in 1942 and by Mr. Herbert Morrison (speaking as Lord President of the Council) at the beginning of 1946. Its structure is "four-storied":

The Problems of the Socialised Sector

1 The *Cabinet* itself is the supreme executive authority under our constitution, and is the final source of decision in the field of economic administration as of any other.

2 The Cabinet must, however, delegate the various divisions of its work to sub-Committees of itself. The Supreme Economic Authority is therefore, in practice, the Economic sub-committee of the Cabinet over which the Lord President presides, and that is known as the *Lord President's Committee*. The members of this Committee are the Ministers mainly responsible for economic affairs ranging from the Chancellor of the Exchequer to the Minister of Town and Country Planning and including, of course, the President of the Board of Trade, the Minister of Labour, the Minister of Fuel and Power, the Minister of Transport, the Minister of Agriculture, and the Minister of Food.

This Committee is advised by a corresponding Official Committee, known as the Steering Committee, of which the Permanent Secretaries of the main economic Departments are members.

3 These two Committees are served by three technical bodies —the *Lord President's Secretariat*, the *Economic Section of the Cabinet Secretariat*, and the *Central Statistical Office*—manned by economists and statisticians who provide information and expert advice.

4 Finally there are the Departments themselves (the Treasury, the Board of Trade, the Ministry of Labour, the Ministry of Fuel and Power, the Ministry of Agriculture, the Ministry of Food, the Ministry of Transport, the Ministry of Works and the Ministry of Town and Country Planning) which are the main executive agents in the economic field, and whose Ministers hold their powers directly from the Crown. Much of their work requires no supervision or checking (other than financial); but they are all, in fact, responsible to the Cabinet, whose authority is delegated to the Lord President's Committee.

This is a complex, but reasonably efficient, instrument of central economic control. Of course, it is impossible to describe the living reality of any system of administrative arrangements and personal relationships in precise words and diagrams. Nevertheless the arrangements described above mean that there are some forty or fifty men and women in Whitehall—Ministers, Civil Servants, economists and statisticians—who are continuously meeting, day after day, in varying groups and Committees who keep under review the economic life of the nation and possess, collectively, great power to influence it. These men compose the Supreme Economic Authority, although the phrase is not used, and it is with their work that we are now chiefly concerned.

By what main problems will these men find themselves faced as the years pass? In the remainder of this chapter, I propose to consider three of them.

Incentives

First, there is the fundamental question of motive or driving force. By what incentives can workers and managers be induced to work hard and efficiently within the socialised sector?

It has long been one of the two main arguments against Socialism that a centrally planned economy, and an egalitarian society, will provide no "economic" motive for labour or risk-taking.

On this subject much confusion has arisen from a failure to distinguish the effect upon economic incentive of central direction on the one hand and the various consequences of economic equality on the other.

The substitution of *central direction* for private enterprise is unlikely to exert any appreciable influence on the distribution of economic incentive.

Incentives—or motives for working hard—may be divided into three groups.

First there are the *positive economic incentives—piece rates* that relate the earnings of the individual directly to productive efficiency; *team bonuses* of various kinds that link his rewards to the output of the group in which he works; and *promotion* up a hierarchy of responsibility and salary scales that provide the main form of economic drive for the professional worker, including the professional manager. All these types of reward are offered to men and women who are employed by others. Profits—the surplus rewards accruing to those who carry the risks of an enterprise—can only influence the efficiency of persons who employ themselves and who both own and manage the profit-making concern. In all other cases profits are paid to legal owners who do not work on the undertaking.

Secondly there are the *negative economic incentives*—the reduction of earnings by fines; the suspension from earnings; and, chief among these punishments, the threat of dismissal or "the sack".

Thirdly there are the *non-economic incentives*—among which it is possible to distinguish (a) the individual's *instinctive impulse* to employ his own productive powers—to "do a good job" and to enjoy social approval by so doing; and the purely *social impulse* to work for the good of the group without any direct advantage to a man or his family.

All these incentives are operating, in a greater or less degree, in our present economic system. Is it possible to say anything about their relative importance?

In general the answer to this question is negative. We are dealing here with some of the deepest questions of human behaviour. We are asking how and why individuals react to changes in their social environment. These are the ultimate problems of individual and social psychology and to my knowledge the necessary scientific work has not yet been done. The investigation of incentive by economists and psychologists is one of the most pressing problems in the whole field of social research and should receive the earliest attention from those responsible for spending money on these subjects. Nevertheless, it is possible to say something on the incentive. In the *first* place I think it is becoming increasingly plain that far too much importance has been attached in the past to purely economic incentives, whether positive or negative. This is a natural mistake in an age that has been saturated with economic thought and in which the great discoveries of economists and economic historians have established a dominant intellectual fashion similar to that enjoyed by the physicist in the nineteenth century. Yet the discoveries made in recent years by psycho-analysts and psychiatrists throw grave doubt upon any assumption that men and women are chiefly influenced by the rational, or even conscious, calculation of their own advantage. It has been shown beyond dispute that we are all moved to action by a set of hereditary impulses that become distorted and perverted by the circumstances and ideas of our early childhood, by the mechanisms of projection and displacement and by our infantile ideas of conscience and cause. It is undoubtedly true that one of these instinctive impulses is that of acquisitiveness—or the search for personal advantage—but it is equally clear that this is only one impulse among many and not necessarily the most important of them. It is almost certain that the impulse to use all one's gifts, and to gain social approval by doing so, is equally powerful. The activity of playing competitive games, and the maintenance of professional standards without immediate reward, are both evidence of this common principle.

In the *second* place it has now been widely demonstrated, in the case of both animals and children, that rewards offer more powerful inducements than punishments. The main triumph of the service of pedagogy, and the chief consequent improvement in the art of teaching, has been to substitute carrots for sticks in our schools. Children learn far more willingly, quickly, happily and permanently in an atmosphere of consideration, interest and reward than they ever did under the shadow of the cane. Horses are more easily "broken in" with lumps of sugar than by the whip. The old circus trainers' boast that "it is all done by kindness" is becoming literally true.

In the *third* place it is important to realise that on any realistic classification of incentives there is no simple opposition between "economic" motives and "social" motives. Many critics of socialism, and some socialists, have written as though the success of a centrally directed economy depended upon the substitution of altruistic "group regarding" objectives for "self regarding" acquisitive impulses. Those who think in this way are almost wholly wrong for a practical reason that I shall state in a moment. But they are also mistaken because they omit from the list of the forces, whose relative importance they attempt to assess, the instinctive forces that may well be the most powerful of all. The efficient economic system will not be one in which private gain is *replaced* by social purposes but one in which the common economic life releases the immensely powerful productive instincts of all individuals, and in which economic rewards are used to reinforce (working with and not against) the rational and moral appreciation of the common good. Full employment, piece rates, and social ownership will,

The Problems of the Socialised Sector

I believe, prove a singularly powerful combination of inducements. Full employment will guarantee free play to all our creative impulses. Piece rates or promotion will enlist our acquisitiveness. Common ownership will show our social conscience. We can and must enjoy the best of these three worlds of human value.

All this is of great importance in understanding the real problems of incentive that will arise in the course of administering the socialised sector. But in considering the use of purely economic incentives *within this sector* and in comparing it with their efficacy under a system of private enterprise there are two further points of great importance.

(*a*) It is obvious that one form of economic incentive—that of "profit-making"—will disappear. But it would be a mistake to suppose that this will affect any large or important group of workers or managers. On the contrary we know that 85 per cent of the "gainfully occupied" persons were employed by other people and not working on their own account before the war. Moreover it is certain that a large number of the remaining 15 per cent were accounted for by shopkeepers and other persons in the distributive trades. It is therefore certain that only a very small proportion of our industrial workers, whether manual or managerial, are directly touched by the incentive of profit or will be affected by its disappearance.

The same conclusion is enforced if one considers the way in which any typical large industrial concern is governed—a railway or a steel works or an aeroplane factory. All the productive physical work is performed by the wage earners—employees of the Corporation. Nine tenths of the management is undertaken by paid managers—also employees of the concern. Most, and in many cases all, of the Directors derive the greater part of their income from their fees—not from their holding of shares in the firm they govern. The only group whose fortunes are affected by the profits that the Company makes are the ordinary and preference shareholders and they do no work for the Company at all. Its efficiency cannot, therefore, be influenced in any serious way by the "profit motive". Indeed, any connection between profits and the maintenance of efficiency has almost wholly disappeared from modern "joint stock" industrial capitalism.

(*b*) The whole question boils down, then, to the use of economic incentives to stimulate the efficiency of *employed* persons. And here it is obvious that there need be no considerable change. All the positive economic incentives—piece rates, team bonuses and promotion within a hierarchy—can be used by any Public Corporation and are already used by some. The Coal Board can continue to pay workers at the coal-face on the basis of the existing (somewhat complex) systems of piece rate earnings; it can maintain the scheme of "pit bonuses" operating in certain collieries, and it must necessarily continue to reward efficient managers by promotion. Indeed, in this last case the opportunities for promotion offered by a unified industry are far greater than those available within any one of the 1,700 firms into which competitive industry has been divided.

It is no doubt true that there will be some reduction in the use of *negative incentives* (economic punishments) in the socialised sector. It will not be so easy to "sack" miners and even the milder forms of discipline—fines and suspensions—will be used more sparingly and administered by Committees on which workers are represented. But we have already seen that no particular harm is likely to come from such a change. Punishments are not particularly efficient methods of influencing human behaviour and it is comparatively easy to start a "virtuous circle" in which kindliness and security, combined with variable rewards, increases the willingness to co-operate and so releases the creative impulses of the normal human being.

From all this it is clear that no particular problems of incentive are raised by the introduction of central direction into an advanced capitalist system. We do not really know to what extent economic incentives matter. But whatever may be the answer to this ultimate question, it is certain that the transfer of large industries from private to public hands need not disturb the distribution of positive economic rewards offered within them to any serious degree. Profits do not accrue to workers or managers. Piece rates and bonuses can be retained. Punishments are relatively ineffective. There is really no problem peculiar to the industries owned by the nation.

It is not quite so simple, however, when we turn from the

effect of central direction to *the effect of economic and social equality* upon the distribution of incentive.

It is obvious that if by "economic equality" were meant a strict arithmetical identity in the rewards offered to all persons (as described by Bernard Shaw in "An Intelligent Woman's Guide to Socialism") then equality so defined would wipe economic incentive off the map. But no one supposes that such a principle of distribution could be established. It satisfies no abstract standard of justice (since it takes no account of need) and it is far removed from the methods of reward that would be acceptable to any large number of organised workers, to whom some differences in payment according to skill and responsibility appear both desirable and right. We must therefore look a little more carefully into the main causes of economic inequality before we can reach any sensible conclusion.

There are three main causes of difference in wealth between individuals:

First there is *inheritance* whereby the children of rich parents receive their property at death and make the wealth so gained the basis for further accumulations. Dr. Dalton has shown in his *Inequality of Income* that this legal right is the main source of large fortunes and the chief reason for the existing inequality in the distribution of income and property.

Secondly there are the broad differences that exist between the rewards offered to the various *occupations*. The professions, including that of industrial and commercial management, are better paid than the manual trades and these traditional differences are the chief source of the present differences in *earned* income.

Since the better paid professions can only be entered after a long and expensive training, these first two causes of economic inequality are closely related to, and reinforce, one another. The relatively rich are better able to meet the cost of making their children into qualified doctors, lawyers, engineers, accountants and university teachers, and thus raising their long-term earning power. Furthermore the immense influence of nepotism, based upon family wealth, in securing all the best paid posts in industry, commerce and finance, is notorious. Hence the possession of property and unearned income begets differences in earned incomes and the resulting differences in total income produce still larger future differences through the right of inheritance. This vicious circle accounts for a large amount of our present inequality and the pattern of society will look very different once it is broken.

Lastly, and least important in the creation of inequality comes the differences in earned income that spring from genuine differences of productivity (i.e. those not associated with the artificial restrictions arising from the necessity for expensive periods of training). Payments by piece rates, differences between the wages of skilled and unskilled workers within an occupation, and promotion up the hierarchy of a corporation or a profession are causes, but relatively unimportant causes, of inequality. Yet it is these differences that are of the greatest importance in raising output.

From this simple analysis a number of important conclusions about the relationship between inequality and incentive can be deduced:

In the *first* place it is clear that the reduction of inequality through a great restriction in the amount of inherited property will actually *increase* the extent to which purely economic incentives are effective. Any change that diminishes the proportion which unearned income bears to earned income in the receipts of any individual will *ipso facto* raise the significance of earned income to him and strengthen his or her desire to *earn* more. This idea can be expressed either in these simple terms or as a complicated proposition about the marginal rates of substitution between income and effort. In either case its truth is amply established by the rapid fall, during the last thirty years, in the number of persons able, or willing, to live without earning; this is a direct result of the severe increase in direct taxation over the same period. Greater equality forces the drones into the ranks of the workers.

In the *second* place it is equally plain that closing the gap between the highly paid professional occupations and manual labour will do little or nothing to diminish the willingness to work in either of these ways of life. The gradual establishment of educational equality will undoubtedly increase the entry into the occupations that are, at present, better paid and held in higher social esteem. When the financial barriers to the

68

acquisition of knowledge and skill are completely broken down, when it costs the individual, boy or girl (or his parents), no more to become a doctor or an economist or an industrial expert than to become a miner or a bricklayer, or a dustman, there will be many more doctors, economists and experts and fewer miners, bricklayers and dustmen. As a result of this movement and in order to prevent it going too far, it will become necessary to pay the existing professions relatively less and the unpleasant manual occupations relatively more. [1] This change is ethically desirable and socially necessary. It represents a movement towards Marshall's economic ideal—that the net advantages of all occupations should be equal.

I am, however, concerned here with the effect of these changes upon economic incentives. Broadly speaking they will have no effect. A man does not work less hard as a doctor seeking promotion within the National Medical Service because the miner is being paid more, even relatively more, than he used to be. A Reader in economics is not less eager to become a professor because the dustman collecting the rubbish from his back door is now getting one third instead of one fifth of what the Reader is receiving. The two sets of payments are not related to one another. Difference of rewards between occupations cannot exert any serious influence upon the desire to secure more within any one of them. Nor can it disturb the desirable rates of recruitment. There will be no shortage of doctors and industrial managers because the manual occupations are relatively better paid since the change in rewards will be chiefly brought about by the pressure of young men and women to enter the professions. The new pattern of relative incomes will be in equilibrium with the true relative scarcities of the varying gifts provided by nature, and the whole arrangement will be more efficient and more just.

The abolition of the unearned element as a main source of personal income, and the establishment of equality in educational opportunity, will then bring most of what we mean by "economic and social equality" without diminishing, in any serious degree, the willingness of men and women to work harder in order to earn more.

[1]The course of the absolute rewards to these occupations will depend upon the pace at which the national income per head is rising. There is no necessity for any set wages or salaries to fall absolutely.

We are now left with the last vital question. If property is equally distributed and the idle *rentier* class disappears, and if all careers are open to the talented without financial let or hindrance, will the differences of income that are of economic value—piece rates and differential rewards for skill and responsibility—be allowed to remain? On this point it is impossible to be dogmatic but two points are worth making.

It would certainly be dangerous to abolish such differentials since no one knows how important they really are. It is true, as I have already shown, that there are good reasons for thinking that their importance has been greatly exaggerated in the past. But they may be of great consequence even so. Common sense, and all the evidence provided by the cases in which time rates are replaced by piece rates, suggest that they are. Now it is obvious that we must seek to preserve any fair method of increasing total output and persuading workers to become more skilled and accept more responsibility. It is thus quite consistent to interpret "equality" to mean the removal of all *unnecessary* sources of inequality—thus leaving room for the maintenance of differences in earned income that promote hard work and the use of all the talents. Such an arrangement is not repugnant to most men's moral judgment. [1]

And certainly, in the second place, there is no evidence that any large group of workers, or socialists, desire any arrangement other than this. No trade union has asked for equality of pay between skilled and unskilled grades or suggested that the bricklayer and his mate, the foreman and the members of his team, should be paid the same weekly wage. Indeed the pressure has been all the other way—to preserve traditional *differences*, even when these have become obsolete and obstructive. The opposition to the establishment of piece rates has usually arisen over the level of the rates and their relationship to the efficiency of new machines, rather than to the principle

[1] The least imprecise definition of what a Socialist means by "economic equality" is to be found in the generally accepted slogan "from each according to his power, to each according to his need". The first half of this ideal is not wholly incompatible with a system of rewards that induces every man and woman to do his best, and it is commonly agreed that the second half—"to each according to his need" —is best secured outside the wage system (by the provision of social services: Family and Income Tax Allowances and the rest). To the Socialist there is a great moral gulf fixed between differences of income that arise from "earnings" on the one hand and inheritance on the other.

itself. Certainly the Labour Party is not committed in any way to the elimination of differences in earned income arising out of genuine differences in productivity.

In all these matters "deeds speak louder than words" and there can be no doubt about what the deeds are. The present schemes for nationalising industries and bringing them into the socialised sector (those for mining, and civil aviation, for example) make full provision for preserving differences of earned income and specify quite large salaries for those carrying the highest administrative responsibilities. "By their fruits ye shall know them"—and there is every sign that one of the consequences of nationalisation will be the establishment, in full force, of the financial incentive that links earnings to productivity, skill and responsibility.

The relationship between "socialism" and economic incentive is then very different from what it is ordinarily supposed to be. The establishment of centralised direction leaves the financial motive for personal efficiency largely unchanged. The whittling away of unearned income increases it. The growth of educational equality will alter relative rewards between occupations without cutting the connection between individual effort and the earnings within each calling. There is every reason for believing that "economic activity" will be so interpreted as to leave ample room for necessary variations in earned income. It is not, therefore, necessary to appeal to new unselfish social impulses to replace the ordinary connection between effort and income. Such impulses may be available. They probably are. They will be welcome in the highest degree. But the fact remains that use can, and will, be made of normal economic motives within the socialised sector and in the new society based upon a planned economy and social equality.

Tactical Control—and the size of the unit of management

The great danger of a centrally directed economy is that of "bureaucracy" and the growth of "red tape". This is the second, and more substantial argument, against planning that we must now examine.

Problems of Economic Planning

Every type of economic system has its own peculiar set of weaknesses. Lack of foresight and inequity are the damning defects of an economic order based upon private enterprise. It is reasonable to suppose that these evils can be overcome by the establishment of a planned economy and the use of taxation to bring about a more equal distribution of property. But unfortunately, no change of institutions is wholly advantageous and centralisation brings another set of administrative problems into the centre of the picture.

The main weakness of large-scale management and excessive centralisation is a certain loss of speed and adaptability.

As concerns grow larger there is a tendency for the time they take to react to changes in their environment to lengthen. Decisions take longer to make and the resistance to change increases disproportionately with the growth in size.

We all know what we mean by "bureaucracy"—the excessive caution and lack of administrative vitality that characterises our Civil Servants, the multiplication of forms and of committees, the eagerness to shelve responsibility and to delay decisions. These weaknesses of our departmental administration have frequently been described. Anyone who has worked for, or in, a large Government department would be the last to deny that there is a real danger that our industries would become paralysed and ineffective if the methods of Whitehall were to be extended to the management of our commercial affairs.

It is, however, essential to distinguish sharply the two main causes of delay and inefficiency in Governmental administration. There is first the question of the Civil Servants themselves (particularly in the Administrative Grade) and then there is the more fundamental problem of the difficulties of large scale administration, as such, whatever its legal form or social purpose.

(a) *The Administrative Grade of the British Civil Service* possesses, as a class, a number of unusual and outstanding virtues. It is intelligent, hard working and honest. But it is composed of men and women, who, for some reason or other, are lacking in "drive" or administrative vitality, who are shy of responsibility and negative in will. Nor does the existing system of promotion bring the best men to the top. Some people attribute these defects to the low average calibre of Cabinet Ministers in the period between the two wars, others to the tendency for rather dull young men to choose a safe and unexciting profession, and yet others to the absence of proper training for the new recruits to the Service, or to the increasing dominance of the Treasury.

We need not, however, trouble much about the historical causes of these evils since their existence is not disputed. It would be disastrous to hand over the administration of any socialised industry to the present generation of established Administrative Civil Servants. They are not the right sort of people. They have not received the right training and most of them are too old to change the character and pace of their work.

Fortunately it is quite unnecessary to contemplate any policy of this kind.

In the *first* place no one intends to hand over industries to Civil Servants at all. Socialised industries are to be run by Public Corporations and these are to possess a great measure of independence. They are to be run by Boards of Control appointed by the Minister. Now there is no conceivable reason why these Boards should contain any large number of men who have been Civil Servants. On the contrary, there is every reason why they should not. The Boards will be chiefly composed of men already experienced in the management of industrial enterprises in general and some of them will be experts in the affairs of the nationalised industry in particular. The Coal Board, for example, contains only one Civil Servant (an exceptionally able man) and is otherwise made up from men who are outstanding experts in the production of coal, or the organisation of labour, or the distribution of coal. There is no question of such a Board being influenced by the practices or traditions of the Civil Service. These men will themselves employ a hierarchy of managers and technical experts and will lay down the terms of employment, and slowly establish the traditions, of an entirely new class of workers—the *Industrial Service of the Public Boards*.

I should be the last person to deny that the formation of this new Service presents us with a series of unsolved problems— of selection, training and incentive—to which there are no cut and dried solutions at present available. Nothing but hard thought, experiment and patience will help us towards a solution of them. But these questions are quite different from that with which we started. The Industrial Service will not be composed of, or directed by, Civil Servants of the present type. That is an entirely unreal fear and the real problems in this field are those already faced, and in part solved, by any existing large industrial undertaking—to which we shall come in the later sections of this chapter.

In the meantime, and in the *second* place, it may be worth stating my personal view that it is easy to see various methods by which the Administrative Grade of the Civil Service could be greatly improved.

The average efficiency of any body of men, charged with an important social duty, can be raised in three ways—by selecting more suitable recruits, by providing them with better training after they have been selected, or by using more trustworthy methods of promotion after they have been trained. All these things can be done in the Administrative Grade of the Civil Service. Better men and women, equally intelligent and possessing greater vitality, can be chosen from among the large number of candidates who offer themselves at the present examinations by making use of the new and far more reliable methods of selection worked out by the War Office Selection Boards during the war. In addition there is every good reason, in my view, to continue the practice whereby a number of older men and women, who have already proved themselves to be capable administrators, are recruited directly to more senior posts in the Service. By these means the inflow of new entrants can be improved and the Service invigorated and freshened by the wider experience of older and successful men.

The training of the selected entrants can be improved out of all knowledge. The programme of training should be based upon two principles: *first* that the young man or woman should work, for a time, in the field for whose administration his or her department is responsible (an official of the Ministry of Education in a school, an official of the Colonial Office in a Colony, an official of the Ministry of Transport on a railway); *second* that at regular intervals in his career the Administrative Civil Servant should be withdrawn from the Service for a period of "sabbatical leave", during which he would be required to refresh his mind, and bring his knowledge up to date, by study and travel. These two provisions secure a practicality and freshness of mind that is notably lacking in the older Civil Servants to-day.

Promotion within the Service should also be reformed in two ways. There should be much more interchange between he various departments in Whitehall, and between the departments as a whole and external Corporations and administrative bodies, in order to secure more varied experience for the senior officers. And there should be less security in the tenure of individual posts without any diminuition in the independence and security of a man's position within the Service as a whole.

These changes taken together would, I am convinced, make a revolutionary improvement in the vigour and capacity of the Service in half a generation. They would add the qualities of vigour, experience and expertness without destroying the virtues of intelligence, loyalty and honesty that the representative Civil Servant already possesses. They would go a long way to adapt the Service to the new, and larger, needs of a changing world and remove from it the reproaches of inactivity and amateurishness that are often, only too often, justified.

(*b*) I must now turn to the more fundamental cause of bureaucracy—*the size of the administrative unit.*

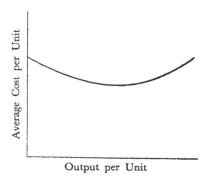

With any given technique of administration the efficiency of a concern is bound to fall off after a certain optimum size has been reached. The economist has always expressed this obvious fact in the form of a U-shaped cost curve for the output of any productive enterprise administered as a single concern—in which all decisions are taken by a single person or governing committee. It is clear that if there is one plant of fixed size (one coal pit or one generating station or one iron foundry), then output cannot be increased beyond a certain point without a disproportionate rise in total cost, since the plant has been constructed for a certain optimum scale of operations. But even if this physical limitation were removed, and the firm became free to build a plant of any size, costs would still be likely to rise, once a certain point had been reached, through the growing inefficiency of its administration. If one committee attempted to manage all the coal pits in the country, or even in one county—i.e., if it tried to centralise all the day-to-day decisions on production, employment and personal relationships into one office—the most hopeless confusion would arise.

The conception of an optimum size, therefore, applies to units of control, as well as to physical plants. A concern can plainly be so small that the modern techniques of management—with cost accountants, personnel departments, quantitative budgeting and production planning—cannot be used at all. Administrative efficiency, therefore, increases for a time with size. But beyond a certain point it declines through congestion and delay. In between these points there is a middle point of maximum efficiency and minimum cost.

It may be worth commenting, in passing, upon the precise reason for the limited size of the administrative optimum. At first sight it might appear that since the duties of management are performed by managers it would be possible to increase indefinitely the size of the concern that could be run efficiently by merely engaging more managers.

I think the explanation of the apparent conflict between fact and theory is to be found by examining the nature of the work to be done by the final and central authority within any organisation that is to work as a unit. The inescapable and peculiar duty of such a person, or committee is that of "co-ordination". This is a terrible word, but it is a real activity. Any organism, whether biological or social, consists of specialised parts carrying out particular duties necessary to the life of the whole. And these parts, or organs, must be directed to a consistent and unified activity by a controlling—or "co-ordinating"—centre.

The human body, for example, consists of arms and legs, eyes and ears, glands and arteries, and if this body is to live and work in a changing world, the activities of sense perception, muscular movement, secretion and circulation must be directed and controlled by a single "co-ordinating" centre—the brain. In the same way a coal pit or a steel factory possess all sorts of specialised organs—teams of manual workers, individual foremen, buying agents, legal experts, purchasing, accounting, planning and personnel departments. All these units within the concern must again be drawn together and their various activities directed to a consistent unity of action by a single authority that appreciates all the changes that affect the life of the concern as a whole. And having considered them, it (the governing centre) must order appropriate and consistent responses to be made by the separate departments since it alone can see the whole picture and bring unity out of diversity.

Now this activity of "co-ordination" increases, and increases disproportionately, with the number of specialised organs and special activities to be "co-ordinated". Take, for example, a concern that only possesses two departments and two departmental chiefs—say a Production Department and a Sales Department with one Production Manager and one Sales Manager. The whole activities of such a firm are covered by, and consultation and cross reference is limited to, a single relationship. There are only two men at the top of the administrative hierarchy to consult with one another; and there is only one relationship (good or bad) between them and their departments. But when there are three departments (say Production, Sales and Finance) then at once there are four such relationships—three between the possible pairs of departments and one between all three departments communicating on matters that concern them all. When the number of departments is increased to four the number of possible relationships—embracing two, three or all four of the departments—rises to *nine*; and when the number of departments rises to five, the number of relationships is *twenty-one*. There is, therefore, a steeply disproportionate increase in the number of cross references, and, therefore, in the amount of "co-ordination" required to keep the activity of these various departments consistent with each other.[1]

No one who has worked in Whitehall can doubt that this is the main source of bureaucratic delay. As I wrote in the *Political Quarterly:*

> "The larger the department, the bigger the State, the more persons must be informed and consulted before a policy can develop consistently. Take an example. Suppose a small firm writes to the Ministry of Supply asking for a continuation of its contract to produce shell-caps or for a licence to extend its machine shop. The difficulty of coming to a decision is much greater than might, at first sight, appear. The Director of the Division for making shell-caps must first pause upon the matter. He will want to know the opinion of his local representative about the record and efficiency of the firm. He must consult the Treasury on the cost of the extension and the proportion to be borne by the Treasury—otherwise money may be wasted or different firms may be offered quite different terms. He must consult the Ministry of Labour to discover whether labour is relatively scarce or relatively abundant in the area in which the firm is situated—otherwise there will be complete confusion (as there often has been) in the geographical distribution of work. He must consult the Ministry of Aircraft Production that they are not going to offer new contracts to this firm— otherwise there will be disastrous competition between Government Departments. He must consult the lawyers of his own Ministry on the legal terms of the contract. Finally he must obtain the sanction of his superior, and of the Planning Department of the Ministry of Supply, and perhaps, if he is especially meticulous, he will also have a word with the Ministry of Production, in order to make sure that this particular increment of shell-caps is consistent with the larger "production plan" of which this programme is a part. But all this "co-ordination" takes time and effort, and I have chosen a particular simple case. Many decisions would require consultations with a dozen, rather than half a dozen, different persons and departments before consistence was secured. All this is inevitable."[2]

What is true of Government Departments must be equally true of any large scale unit of administration or business

---

[1] This proposition can, of course, be expressed in a simple mathematical formula.
[2] *Political Quarterly*, 1944, pp. 107–8.

organisation. Beyond a certain size, or degree of complexity, it gets tied up and partly paralysed in the elaborate arrangements necessary to keep every one informed of what everyone else is doing.

This somewhat abstract argument has an immediate practical lesson for those who are responsible for organising the socialised sector. It is essential that they should distinguish sharply between the advantages of economic planning and central direction on the one hand, and those of large scale administration on the other. The extent to which efficiency can be increased by enlarging the size of the unit to be administered as a single concern are strictly limited. In very few cases will it amount to any large fraction of a modern industry. Take coal for example. No doubt the present scale of management is too small. Roughly, 3,000 pits are administered by 1,700 firms. The number of firms is too large and much can be gained by grouping them and developing larger and more specialised managerial teams. But it would be absurd to suppose that all the pits in the industry should be administered from one centre ("mining from Whitehall") or even all the pits in one district or county. Between these two limits there is an optimum number of pits that can be merged successfully into one efficient group. Only an expert could say how large this number is likely to be. But it is certain to be far short of the number contained in the industry or in any of the larger districts, so that an efficient organisation of the industry will demand the maintenance of a number of semi-independent managements and the delegation to them of substantial powers. The same principle will apply to iron and steel, to road transport, and to civil aviation. There are already signs—in the provision for Regional Boards and delegated powers in the Coal Mines Act and in the creation of more than one Operating Company in the field of Civil Aviation—that the essential truth of this doctrine is fully appreciated by those now responsible for the organisation of the socialised sector.

At first sight it may be thought that there is some logical conflict between asserting that central direction is a more efficient method of running our economic life and recognising that there is a strict limit to the size of the efficient concern. This, however, is not so. The truth of the matter lies in the distinction drawn in military matters between strategy and tactics; i.e., between the control of an army throughout a campaign and the conduct of day-to-day administration and actual fighting. In the larger field of strategy the relationships between infantry and artillery, fighting forces and supply, land and air, one battle and the next, must be foreseen, planned and controlled from the top to the bottom of the hierarchy and from the beginning to the end of both the battle and the war. But it is an equally urgent necessity, to preserve flexibility, decisiveness, speed and spirit in the smaller units during the actual course of each day's fighting. This problem has only been solved in the fighting Services by increasing both the extent of communications between the fighting units and their headquarters (and therefore the potential degree of unity and control) on the one hand, and the independence and degree of authority left to the commanders in the field on the other. This paradoxical logic is the complex necessity of any co-operative action.

Exactly the same distinction applies to economic activity. There are strategic issues of the first importance in the economic life of the nation—the relations between industry and industry, output and purchasing power, consumption and investment, change and security, work and leisure, education and industrial demand. There are the large reactions of the nation's economy to the changing conditions of domestic and international demand, of the technique of production and of political conditions at home and abroad. In all these matters it is the strategic principle that is dominant. A swift, complex, and yet consistent response by the total economy is required. The whole must be seen in the parts and the end from the beginning. At the other end of the story are the requirements of efficient tactics. Every factory, every shop, and every local branch of a bank has a hundred daily problems to face and decisions to take. Raw materials must be ordered, the load on machines must be decided, finished products must be marketed, hands must be engaged, promotions must be made, discipline must be enforced, new techniques must be introduced. All these endless decisions should be taken wisely and carefully, but above all, quickly. No decision, or a late decision, is frequently worse than a bad decision. These are the problems of "in-fighting" and to solve them the local commanders—the immediate managers of socialised mines and foundries and bus services— must hold extensive delegated powers. No doubt the exact division of powers between the Supreme Economic Authority, the Public Boards of the socialised industries, and the managers working in the field is a subject of great difficulty and complexity, and one that I cannot pursue through lack of space. Nevertheless the principle is clear and the lesson plain. Local initiative must be preserved, and even increased,[1] in an economy increasingly subject to central direction.

This double development may appear paradoxical but it is not self-contradictory. On the contrary it is essential for any group of men and women who have a complex task to perform, in the execution of which they must divide themselves into a number of specialised working parties, that they should combine unity and consistency with speed in their common action. This can only be done by increasing the degree of central direction without losing the power of local decision. "Unity in diversity" is the clue to riches in the material, as well as in the spiritual, universe.

Strategic Control—By Prices and Costs

We now come to a more philosophical question that has greatly interested economists in recent years.[2] What general ends should a planned economy serve?

Two of the main objectives of policy are obvious. It is essential to preserve *full employment* if our wealth is to be maximised, and to keep our *balance of payments* in equilibrium at the level required by full employment. These two problems are, however, the subject matter of preceding chapters, and I shall assume that they have been solved.

If we have been successful in keeping all our men and

[1]The use of this word is not a mere rhetorical exaggeration, since in many capitalist concerns the local managers are responsible to Boards sitting in London despite the fact that the companies may not be very large. Their properties are widely scattered and sometimes linked to other, largely irrelevant, activities. In such cases central direction could be used to increase, rather than decrease, the degree of *local* autonomy.

[2]The treatment of this subject is necessarily more technical than what I have so far written. Any reader not familiar with the jargon of economics will probably do best to turn on to the simple conclusion on page 88.

machines at work and if we have secured the necessary food and raw materials from abroad, the next central problem is that of *relative* production. What commodities should be produced and in what quantities?

In this matter I am an unrepentant believer in the principle of "consumer's sovereignty". Given that production is at a maximum and that we are using the instrument of taxation to bring about a more equal distribution of income and property, I see every reason that the consuming public should be free to spend the income left to them as they please and to determine, by so doing, the relative output of consumption goods to suit themselves. No good argument has ever been advanced for abandoning this form of economic democracy.

It has always been alleged that the ability to give consumers what they want is one of the great advantages of a private enterprise economy. Those of us who are democratic socialists believe that a planned economy will be more technically efficient for the achievement of *any* set of chosen ends. If this is the case, it must follow that central direction can be used to satisfy consumers' preferences and thus retain the plain advantage of providing people with what they want. Again, planning and liberty are compatible and we should do our utmost to enjoy the best of both these worlds.

It is, of course, perfectly consistent with the principle of consumers' sovereignty that some of the most important services should be provided communally—defence, education, housing and social security. It is wholly reasonable that the consuming public should choose to satisfy certain of its wants through the provision, by the State, of services financed out of taxation. But when these have been paid for, a certain tax-free income will remain in the hands of consumers who can, and should be, left free to spend this money as they please. And the programme of production, outside the limited field of socialised consumption, should be guided by their wishes.

The method by which this end is achieved in an economy based on private enterprise is familiar. The consumer puts prices upon the goods sold in the final retailer's market. Competing producers are forced to buy the necessary labour, capital and material at prices that tend to equal the value of the additional physical product for which the last increment of the factor in question is responsible; and competition further leads to the variations in the output of each commodity that will keep prices equal to the costs of production, allowing for a normal rate of return to risk-bearing. This is the main purpose and result of the capitalist system of prices and costs—at least in the absence of monopoly.

Do these principles of pricing apply to the planned economy? Is this instrument of measurement and guidance available to our Supreme Economic Authority?

Clearly it is. This proposition can be demonstrated at two levels of reasoning.

In *technical* terms it can be shown that the whole theory of value (the theoretical analysis of the nature and consequences of the pricing system) has been based in recent years on two assumptions—that there is a scarcity of resources and that consumers possess an ordered system of preferences. Neither of these conditions is in any way affected by the substitution of central direction for private enterprise in the taking of economic decisions. The logic of pricing and costing therefore applies as much, or as little, to a planned economy as to any other.

In *practical* terms it is equally obvious that pricing and costing can be used in the socialised sector. Consumers can plainly be left free to spend their money as they please. Boards of Public Corporations can be instructed to keep records of the costs of production and to pay for labour, capital and raw materials approximately the value, as shown in the free consumer's market, of the goods produced by the marginal in-put of the factors used. The Supreme Economic Authority has then only to issue a general instruction that outputs should be adjusted to the levels that will bring these prices and costs into rough equality with one another for the problem to be solved.

It is, let me say at once, possible to use costing systems with varying degrees of accuracy. The Russians, for example, make no charge in their accounts for the use of land or fixed capital by socialised trusts. They merely require the trusts to pay their way, to make a contribution to the central exchequer roughly proportionate to their size, and to meet the costs of the labour and raw materials which they employ. The Boards of Control are, therefore, not allowed to finance a deficit by a continuous increase in short term borrowings from the socialised banking system. All this is very crude, and we may think it wise to include more of the true costs to society of industrial production —including the use of land and the replacement of fixed capital —and to refine the system of accountancy to the point at which the further expenditure of time and effort on making elaborate calculations ceases to be worth while. But it is obvious that such rules can be made, and accounts of any degree of refinement can be kept. There is no difficulty about it and the principle that such accounts should be kept has, in fact, been included in the provisions of the Coal Mines (Nationalisation) Act.

The only serious problem in this field arises under a different head. What is the *correct instruction* to give the Public Corporations operating in the socialised sector? This question has given rise to a good deal of controversy among economists in recent years.

The problem can be simply stated. The strictly logical directive that should be given to all managements runs as follows: "Produce at the level of output where the price of the commodity you are producing is equal to the *marginal* cost of production."

This is the correct instruction since the real cost to society of the last increment of the output of any commodity is the additional in-puts of labour, material, capital and management required to make it. The value of these in-puts makes up the marginal cost of production to the socialised industry, and equilibrium requires that the price of any output should just cover the social costs attributable to it. If this condition is not fulfilled, the value of the additional products that can be produced by the same labour, or land, or capital on other employments will exceed the value created by their use in this particular industry and society will gain by moving the factor in question to the higher margin. This is the familiar conclusion of the traditional theory of value.

The correct directive can be applied with great simplicity to a socialised industry in which there are many production units. Take *coal*, for example. Technical conditions make it inevitable that hundreds of separate mines should continue in operation. For each of these mines there will be an optimal level of output for which average costs are at a minimum. To raise either more or less coal from the pit will increase the average cost per ton. At this point of minimum average cost the additional or marginal cost will be equal to the average cost —since the latter is neither rising nor falling. If the output of the industry has, in the meantime, been kept at the level where the demand price for coal will just cover average costs—then price will be equal to marginal cost also. The receipts of the socialised industry, and of each production unit within it, will be equal to both average and marginal costs, including the general level of return on the industrial capital (owned by the State) which has been invested in the industry.

Equilibrium for the industry is reached when the number of mines kept in operation together produce an output whose demand price is equal to the minimum average cost and therefore the marginal cost of production.

All this gives rise to no great difficulty. But the position is more complicated, unfortunately, when the technical conditions allow only one plant to operate. There cannot, for instance, be hundreds of railway systems or electrical grids. There can only be one in each case and it is most unlikely that the conditions of demand will enable the railway or the generating stations to operate at the point where average costs are at a minimum and therefore equal to marginal costs. This can only happen by accident and in most cases, and at most times, the railway system or the generating stations will be required to operate at a point either before, or after, the technical optimum has been reached. If the railway system is carrying less traffic than could be carried at the lowest average cost, it will be working at a point where average costs are falling (a condition of "increasing returns") and at which, therefore, additional or marginal cost is *below* the average cost. If the railway is working beyond the point of minimum average cost (in a condition of "decreasing returns"), average costs are rising and marginal costs are *above* average costs. In neither case is it possible for the price of transport to be equal to both marginal and average costs.

A clear-cut and inescapable choice now emerges. Should the socialised industry, operating a single plant, be instructed to produce the output at which price is equal to marginal cost or the output at which price is equal to average cost?

There is no doubt about the right *theoretical* answer. [1] The marginal directive should be enforced. The cost of the in-puts of labour and material to the railway system, or to the electrical generating station, is measured by the marginal cost of each increment of output. Prices should therefore cover these costs and only these costs—no less and no more.

But despite the accuracy of this reasoning I am convinced that it would be a grave mistake for the Supreme Economic Authority to issue any such directive. It could only result in confusion for two very obvious reasons:

In the *first* place it would reduce the status of accountancy and the principle of accountability to empty formularies. It would bring the finances of a semi-independent Public Corporation into confusion. In the case of a railway called upon to operate under conditions of falling costs, or increasing returns, the marginal directive would require the railway to maintain the price of transport services below their average cost.

Hence the railway's receipts would be below its average costs and it would make a loss, and perhaps a very large loss, however energetic or efficient its workers or management might be. If, on the other hand, the state of the demand for transport required the railways to operate under conditions of decreasing returns, the marginal directive would enable the railways to make large profits, however lazy and incompetent the operatives might become.

It is surely obvious that an arrangement of this kind is quite unworkable. If managers and workers can make large surpluses, or appear responsible for large deficits, without any change in their application or efficiency, the set of accounts by which they are supposed to be guided will become meaningless and irritating to them. Those who work in concerns making

---

[1]At least this has always been assumed by theoretical economists writing on this subject. But Mr. Coase has just published a very convincing Article (*The Marginal Cost Controversy, Economist,* 1946), in which he argues that making price equal to a falling marginal cost is not even the correct theoretical policy. Mr. Coase states that if average costs are falling because of the existence of a fixed overhead cost that the correct pricing policy is a *two part tariff*—requiring a fixed contribution to the overhead from each consumer and then a price for output equal to marginal variable cost. By this means marginal price is kept equal to cost, while, at the same time, total costs are covered. This conclusion greatly strengthens my general contention, although giving it a much more subtle interpretation. Mr. Coase's article appeared too late for me to include a consideration of it in the main text.

large "profits" will expect increased wages, while managers and workers condemned, through no fault of their own, to make endless "losses" will become discouraged by the hopelessness of their position and debauched by the right to draw unlimited and unearned subsidies from the public purse. If the keeping of accounts is to be taken seriously, and if the handling of public funds is to be treated as an important social responsibility, then the formal logic of the marginal directive must be discarded.

In the *second* place, the consistent application of the marginal directive would reduce price policy to confusion. So far we have assumed that the rate of in-put of the factors of production, and consequently the rate at which average and marginal costs are running, are constant over time, but this they certainly are not. On the contrary, capital and replacement expenditure is undertaken at all sorts of regular and irregular intervals. Machines may be replaced once a year or once in five years. Buildings may be restored or rebuilt at any time. Pure logic requires that only current costs—or to-day's in-puts—should be considered in fixing to-day's prices, and that during the periods in which no current replacements are being made these "fixed" assets and the need to restore them should be wholly ignored. Present marginal costs, to which price should logically be equal, exclude every cost that need not (at the moment) be paid. Non-recurrent expenditure should only be taken into account when it is made. Prices should consequently only cover the current cost of hiring the factors of production that (unlike the "fixed" assets) have an immediate alternative use in other industries.

All this reasoning is strictly consistent with itself. Unfortunately any attempt to apply it in practice would produce fantastic results. Consider a socialised railway system. On any given day the cost, in the above sense, of carrying an additional passenger would be zero. There would be empty seats and the marginal cost of filling them would be nothing. Current "in-puts" would be nothing—no more drivers or porters or coal would be needed. Hence marginal costs would be zero and transport would be free. As an immediate consequence the railways would become congested and extra trains would have to be organised. The cost of these extra trains would be true costs, involving a current increase in the use of labour and fuel, and prices would have to be raised at once to cover them. Empty places would then appear once more and fares would again disappear. Furthermore on any day that any decision has to be taken to replace engines or rolling stock, fares must be sharply increased to cover these current capital costs, with the immediate consequence that empty seats reappear and fares must be reduced to zero once again. [1]

It is in order to avoid this absurd and disastrous instability of prices that cost calculations should include an estimate of all the future payments that can be foreseen—those made necessary by the replacement of machinery, the reconstruction of buildings, and the long term training of skilled workers, as well as those arising from the immediate employment of labour and the current consumption of materials. All these make up the long period social cost of maintaining a steady flow of output and should be covered by the prices charged for the product.

The result of all this reasoning is comfortingly simple. Industries and production units within the socialised sector must be guided by a system of prices and costs if consumers are to retain authority over them. It is only common sense to recognise that independent managements (and the workers organised by them) will not take accounts seriously, or be restrained by financial responsibility, unless it is possible for them to balance their budgets. To make this possible it is

---

[1] The truth is that the distinction drawn between "short" and "long period" costs in past theoretical discussion has been illogical and misleading. All the relevant average and marginal cost curves are based upon estimates of *future* cost. It is quite irrelevant to ask *when* these costs are to be incurred (except for the purpose of introducing the quantitatively unimportant subtleties of discounting). In a continuous process of production all the costs of replacement will fall due and should be allowed for (with appropriate discounting rates) in the calculations of current costs and cost schedules. The moment that this point is realised all difficulty disappears. All depreciation allowances and maintenance charges should be included—since they are anticipated future charges—and the only factors of production that should be left out of the commitments are those which are quite specific to the industry in question and yet which require no maintenance at all. Such factors are non-existent or very rare—see articles in *Economic Journal* for 1936 by Mr. A. P. Lerner and myself. The only logical alternative to the common-sense practice of including all the costs that can be foreseen in current estimates would be to include the whole cost of each capital item in the period in which it was actually incurred. But such a policy would lead to the fantastic fluctuations of price shown to be impracticable in the text above. The error in the past has sprung from the failure to realise that the relevant cost curves are estimates of future costs including replacement charges, and an inability to see that reasonable price stability is an essential condition of economic activity.

essential that output, in industries containing both many production units and only one, should be kept at the level where prices cover average costs. All costs, long period and short period, fixed and variable, current and replacement, should be included in the estimates upon which prices are based.

The correct directive should be given to the socialised Corporations by the Supreme Economic Authority is then very simple and falls into three parts—"First establish an accurate system of forward costing. Secondly include in it all the payments, however distant, that can be reasonably foreseen. Thirdly, vary output so as to make prices cover average costs. If demand falls so much that you cannot cover these costs by any variation in output open to you, then, but only then, shall we consider reducing your fixed capital charges." By this means a large degree of automatic guidance can be given to the Corporations without any sacrifice in the power of the central directorate.[1]

The strategic objective of production will then be secured—to give consumers what they want.

Conclusion

Space forbids me to say more. I have only been able to touch upon three of the problems that will face the Supreme Economic Authority, in administering the socialised sector—and about these I have argued that it should seek to preserve consumers' sovereignty and the objective measurement of opportunity lost by using an accurate pricing system; that it should retain an optimum size for the unit of industrial management in each socialised industry; and that, while removing the inequalities arising from unearned income and restricted educational opportunity, it should preserve differences of earned income at least until it has been conclusively shown that they are not a necessary form of incentive.

It would be idle to pretend that this is an exhaustive list of the vital tasks that must be undertaken by the Authority. I have

[1]In addition to this directive on output and accounting policy it will, of course, be necessary for the Supreme Economic Authority to issue an instruction that maximum technical efficiency (and therefore minimum average costs) are achieved, and to follow up this directive by objective and comparative tests. But this raises another large question that I can only list in the next and concluding section.

not been able to mention four of the most important of them—the need to adopt the modern scientific methods of personnel selection and vocational guidance to distribute the working population between occupations and grades; the use of relative wages rates to aid the movement of labour from industry to industry; the spread of modern forms of personnel management; and the adaptation of the principles of cost accountancy and the direct measurement of industrial efficiency to the industrial concerns working in the socialised sector. Some of these questions have been raised in other articles and I must leave the expression of my own views about them to a future publication.[1]

I have one last reflection to offer. Those of us who support the present Labour Government are engaged in a great social experiment. We believe that it is possible to build up an economic order by democratic methods that is both more efficient and more just than that it replaces; more efficient because the methods of science (observation, logic and conscious control) can be used in a planned economy and because a larger proportion of our talent can be discovered, trained and suitably employed by an egalitarian society; more just because it will abolish inequalities that correspond neither to service nor merit. We believe that we now lead the British people in their ancient practice of adapting traditional institutions to the slow growth of knowledge and virtue.

Nevertheless this hope of ours is a belief. It is not knowledge. We cannot be certain that we are right. We must therefore keep our eyes open and our minds fresh. We must learn from our mistakes and escape from the slavery of fixed ideas. And it is comforting to reflect that if we are wrong the supreme virtue of our democratic practice can assert itself and substitute other ideas in our place. No Government, no doctrine, no Party, lives forever in the changing affections of British people.

In the meantime we must bend our energies, temporary holders of a popular sovereignty, to the slow creation of the reformed society in which we rest our domestic hope.

[1]To the book on the *Economics of Democratic Socialism* that I still hope some day to write.

Paper V

PROFESSOR HAYEK ON
ECONOMIC PLANNING

*In 1944 Professor Hayek published his "Road to Serfdom" in which he
set forth the extreme liberal case against economic planning and advanced
his main contention that it was bound to lead to political dictatorship.
The following year I published the following reply in the "Economic
Journal". In it I attempt to show that his argument rests upon a false
conception of the term "planning" and that the historical development
of this country does not support his views. I also raise the larger problem
of the relation between reason and social policy.*

*I imagine that Professor Hayek would hold that some of the policies
pursued by the Labour Government and particularly the restoration of,
in 1947, some power to direct labour, justify his fears. I, on the other
hand, would point to the maintenance and extension of political democracy
over the same period. The reader must judge the merits of the argument
for himself.*

PROFESSOR HAYEK published, last year, a sincere, eloquent, and influential work entitled *The Road to Serfdom*, in
which he set forth the relationship that he believes to exist
between economic planning and political dictatorship. The
purpose of the present article is to explain the grounds upon
which I, and other democratic Socialists, reject his powerful
plea to abandon our beliefs in the institutions of a planned
economy.

2 Both we and he seem agreed about the ends of economic
and social policy. As Professor Hayek rightly says, "There can
be no doubt that most Socialists here still believe profoundly in
the liberal idea of freedom" (p. 23). We all wish to live in a
community that is as rich as possible, in which consumers' preferences determine the relative output of goods that can be
consumed by individuals, and in which there is freedom of discussion and political association and responsible government.

We are all "individualists" in the sense that we all want to see the restrictions placed upon personal liberty reduced to the minimum required to prevent one man's freedom from destroying another's. We all reject the modern regression to authoritarian government and the excessive worship of collective consciousness.

We differ radically, however, about the means by which these ends can best be secured. Professor Hayek believes that the pursuit of equality and the growth of economic planning will lead to the regimented and cruel society that we all want, more than anything else, to avoid. Socialist economists believe exactly the opposite. Most of us are socialist in our economics because we are "liberal" in our philosophy, and we believe that it is Professor Hayek who has missed the road to freedom that all humanitarian "liberals" wish to find.

3 I should like, first, to state Professor Hayek's argument as I understand it, and then criticise it.

Professor Hayek's central thesis consists, if I understand it aright, of four propositions—from which he believes that certain consequences follow.

The *first* of these propositions is that the course of history and the development of national character are largely determined by the life and death of ideas. Thus Professor Hayek says:

> ". . . though for the time being the different ideals are represented [in this war] by hostile nations fighting for their existence, we must not forget that this conflict has grown out of a struggle of ideas within what, not so long ago, was a common European civilisation . . ." (p. 8).

And again:

> "That a change of ideas, and the force of human will, have made the world what it is now, though men did not foresee the results, and that no spontaneous change in the facts obliged us thus to adapt our thought, is perhaps difficult for the English to see, just because in this development the English have, fortunately for them, lagged behind most of the European peoples" (p. 9).

Thus the main source of change and of the great catastrophes in history is to be found, according to Professor Hayek, in the free acceptance or rejection of "ideas" (i.e., social theories and moral judgments) by the governing groups of the time.

Secondly, Professor Hayek goes on to say that the only "idea" upon which political liberty has safely rested in the past is that of economic liberty or freedom of enterprise—by which term Professor Hayek appears to mean the recognition in law, and the active preservation by law, of the right of the individual to do what he likes with his labour and property.

> "We have progressively abandoned that freedom in economic affairs without which personal and political freedom has never existed in the past" (p. 10).

Professor Hayek is at pains to explain (pp. 13–14) that he does not wish to defend unchanging institutions or support mere inactivity on the part of the State. *Laissez-faire* is not enough. He wishes to see the State continuously active in preserving economic freedom, in scotching monopoly or syndicalism wherever it may appear, and in saving the economically weak from destruction by the strong.

Then, *thirdly*, Professor Hayek says that the opposite and, indeed, the only alternative to the "idea" of economic freedom so defined is the "idea" or policy of economic planning in a particular form:

> "What our planners demand is a *central direction of all economic activity according to a single plan*, laying down how the resources of society should be 'consciously directed' to serve particular ends in a particular way" (p. 26).

And, as we shall see, this is the essential step in Professor Hayek's argument.

From this point Professor Hayek goes on to argue, in the *fourth* place, that planning of this kind must be based upon an agreement about ends (a common moral judgment) that is lacking in any human society of which we know, and that the disillusionment following the successive failures of the Planning Authority to implement any "plan" capable of satisfying all individuals and groups within the planned society will lead to a growing faith in, and demand for, political dictatorship. This argument, complicated and speculative though it may seem, is unquestionably that upon which Professor Hayek rests his case:

> ". . . But where all the means to be used are the property of society, and are to be used in the name of society according to a unitary plan, a 'social' view about what ought to be done must guide all decisions . . . [this] attempt to direct all economic activity according to a single plan would raise innumerable questions to which the answer could be provided only by a moral rule, but to which existing morals have no

answer and where there exists no agreed view on what ought to be done . . ." (p. 43).

". . . The inability of democratic assemblies to carry out what seems to be a clear mandate of the people will inevitably cause dissatisfaction with democratic institutions. Parliaments come to be regarded as ineffective 'talking shops', unable or incompetent to carry out the tasks for which they have been chosen . . ." (p. 46).

". . . Yet agreement that planning is necessary, together with the inability of democratic assemblies to produce a plan, will evoke stronger and stronger demands that the Government, or some single individual, should be given powers to act on their own responsibility . . ." (p. 50).

Such is the essence of Professor Hayek's argument.

From it, and assuming it to be true, Professor Hayek draws a series of horrific conclusions in the remainder of his book. The all-embracing "plan" must be enforced by arbitrary administrative decision, so the "rule of law" will disappear (Chap. VI). Consumers' sovereignty, the free choice of occupation, and the right to independent moral judgments must all be sacrificed (Chap. VII). The disappearance of property leads to the direct determination of the individual's wealth and status by the dictatorial political power (Chap. VIII). The reaction against democracy brings the worst people into power, with the concentration camp and the torture chamber as their favourite instruments of government, and the growth of collectivism releases and inflames the evil passions of the people (Chap. X). [1] In order to "make the plan work", all citizens must be coerced or deceived into making the same moral judgments, so that freedom of thought and objective science must be stamped out (Chap. XI); and with the final conquest of authoritarian rule, the possibility of a moral life disappears.

Thus, concludes Professor Hayek, any departure from the practice of free enterprise, any hope that reason and science

---

[1]There is a curious arbitrariness in the assumptions that Professor Hayek makes in different parts of the book about the psychological forces at work in individuals and societies. Some of them are very nearly contradictory. At one point Professor Hayek speaks of ". . . the craving for freedom . . ." as ". . . the strongest of all political motives . . ." (p. 19). Yet later on in the book he swings to the other extreme: ". . . it seems to be almost a law of human nature that it is easier for people to agree on a negative programme, on the hatred of an enemy, on the envy of those better off, than on any positive task . . ." (p. 103). Professor Hayek finds it difficult to make up his mind whether the deepest impulses of human beings are good or bad. It is a pity that Professor Hayek makes no use of the light that has been thrown upon these matters by scientific inquiry in recent years; and remains content with old-fashioned and unsupported, yet dogmatic, generalisations about human nature and emotional behaviour.

may be applied to the direction of economic activity, any attempt at economic planning, must lead us remorselessly to serfdom—to the government of sadists and gangsters, down to the horrible road that the Germans have travelled, to a strait jacket of frenzy and evil.

4 I wish to make three criticisms of Professor Hayek's complex thesis.

In the *first* place, I suggest that Professor Hayek has not asked himself with sufficient determination what he means by the phrase "economic planning", and that in escaping this obligation of logic he has been led to neglect all recent writings on the subject and to hammer heavily upon an open door.[1]

If by "economic planning" is meant the imposition of a complete budget of production upon the community in which the output of every commodity, from power plants to razor-blades, is laid down for years ahead, in which the occupation and distributive share of every citizen are determined by a central authority over which he has no ultimate control and on which he can exert no influence either as a producer or a consumer—then I quite agree with him that a régime of this kind could only be fettered upon us by dictatorship and terror.

But Professor Hayek should know that, rightly or wrongly, this is not what most of us now mean by "economic planning". We use that term to indicate a *principle of administration and not an inflexible budget of production*. Over ten years ago I wrote:

> "It is . . . necessary to be clear about two different uses to which the machinery of centralised control may be put. Planning does not in the least imply the existence of *a* Plan—in the sense of an arbitrary industrial budget which lays down in advance the volume of output for different industries. Planning does not, and should not, imply any dogmatism about the future. It is not possible to tell in detail what will happen to human tastes, to technical invention, to general standards of security and wellbeing. It would therefore be foolish in the extreme to attempt to lay down plans which could not be amended quickly in the light of changing social requirements. . . .
>
> "What then is the true characteristic of planning? If it does not involve the construction of a single plan . . . what is the correct definition of its essential nature? The element common to all the

---

[1]It is of interest to note that Professor Hayek makes only one reference to the work of those of us who are both practising economists and also Socialists, and that in a footnote. His only modern references are to the students of government and sociology, while his most recent Socialist economists are Marx, Engels, Shaw and the Webbs!

forms of new control we regard as 'Planning' is the extension in the size of the unit of management and the consequent enlargement of the field surveyed when any economic decision is taken. . . . All forms of planning machinery extend the area of economic life surveyed by the deciding authority and increase the number and importance of the economic quantities that can be controlled by someone."[1]

From this passage it is perfectly clear that what I, and other democratic socialists, have in mind when we advocate the practice of economic planning is the creation of an economic system in which:

(*a*) The final responsibility for taking economic decisions is transferred from the private company or group of shareholders to the representatives of the community sitting upon the Board of a Public Corporation—who are, in their turn, answerable to some Supreme Economic Authority dependent upon a Parliament freely elected by the people.

(*b*) But that the economic system so administered need not be used to implement any "plan" in the sense of a rigid programme of production arbitrarily determined. The Supreme Economic Authority need not be directed by Parliament to impose any programme of production and consumption upon the community—any more than it itself imposes a rigid programme of political action without continuous reference to the state of public opinion. On the contrary, the centrally directed economy can be, and should be, instructed to adapt its programme to the changing wishes of the consuming public and the changing conditions of technical efficiency. Indeed, we have sought to demonstrate the possibility, and advocate the desirability, of using a pricing and costing system to guide the decisions of the Planning Authorities:

". . . there is no formal or logical contradiction between planning and pricing. It is perfectly possible for a centralised authority to order a price system to appear and to follow the guidance it necessarily gives. *There is no necessary connection between the form of the authority by which decisions are taken and the principles according to which the decisions are made. . . .*"[2]

What we therefore have in mind is a new method of taking economic decisions, a new principle of economic administration,

[1]Durbin, "The Importance of Planning", *New Trends in Socialism* (1935), pp. 149–150 (quoted above, pp. 43-4).
[2]*Op. cit.*, p. 155 (quoted above, p. 48).

and not the imposition of any economic tyranny upon a free society.

Professor Hayek must be aware of the thought that has been given in recent years by economists who are also Socialists to the methods by which a "planned economy" could preserve conscious choice and make use of prices and costings to that end. It is, of course, perfectly proper for Professor Hayek to hold that we have not solved these problems to his satisfaction, but it is not reasonable of him to write as though we used the phrase to mean budgeted production when it is plain, beyond dispute, that we are speaking of centralised administration.

5 Yet the distinction is vital. By "economic planning", I repeat, we mean a *change in the direction of responsibility*. Instead of looking towards small and unrepresentative minorities of shareholders, the persons or Corporations directing production would look upwards, or towards a Central Economic Authority, for guidance on the larger questions of output, prices, investments and costs. I am perfectly aware that a great number of arguments have been advanced against "economic planning" of this kind—that it will be "bureaucratic" or inefficient, that it will lack incentives, that it will not save. And Socialist economists are perfectly prepared to meet these arguments one by one. But this is not the vital matter in dealing with Professor Hayek's thesis—since he gives no consideration whatever to this meaning of the term. If "planning" means a method of economic administration, and not a comprehensive programme of economic activity, if "economic planning" involves no "economic plan" in Professor Hayek's sense, then all his arguments against "planning" fall to the ground.

Nor is it open to Professor Hayek to complain that this is a paradoxical use of terms, since the apostles of "free enterprise" have continuously argued that their "unplanned economy" is not, in any important sense, "unplanned". Indeed, the choice of words is unimportant as long as they are used to clarify rather than to confuse the argument.

To make the point fully clear it is perhaps necessary to make one further distinction. It is, of course, one of the great advantages of a "planned economy", in my sense of the term, that it is possible to construct *statistical budgets* of production for long periods ahead—to say, for example: we shall need 4 million new houses in the next ten years, and the execution of this housing programme will need x bricklayers and y standards of timber and z tons of steel; or to calculate that an adequate nutritional programme will require the production, by British farmers, of x tons of beef and y gallons of milk. One of the superiorities of a centrally directed economy will be this ability to analyse and add up, to calculate and foresee, the statistical implications of any given decision—and in this sense there will be many industrial "plans" that can be combined in order to give a statistical picture or budget of the productive activity of society as a whole. But all this has nothing to do with Professor Hayek's "plans" and "budgets", because there is nothing arbitrary or inflexible about the statistical programmes just described. These "plans" are drawn up only in order to implement, and work out the "logistics" (as the Americans would say), of preferences freely indicated by the consumer in the markets for consumption goods and capital goods that we assume to exist. And if any inconsistency is discovered, or a change takes place later, in the tastes and preferences of the consumer, then the "plans" can be altered to suit the new conditions. They are neither sacrosanct nor authoritative. If the public finds that it wants less houses, or more gramophones, then the "plans" can be changed, for they possess no validity in themselves, and it is inconceivable that we should be dragooned or terrorised into obeying a set of figures drawn up for the sole purpose of giving us what we want.

Let me take a single example of what I mean. Suppose a decision is taken to make the iron and steel industry subject to "economic planning". The fundamental difference between "planning" in Professor Hayek's sense and mine is at once apparent. In Professor Hayek's sense of the term this would mean that the Planning Authority would lay down a detailed programme for the production of bars, plates, angles, billets, blooms, nuts and bolts for a number of years ahead, it would decide the uses to which these products should be put, and so dictate the consumption of all steel-using consumers' goods, it would conscript the necessary number of workers to man the industry and direct them to live in certain places and work for certain wages. In order to force them into obedience, it would have to liquidate the Trade Unions and consign the shop stewards and the workers' political leaders to the concentration camp, the torture chamber, and the shooting squad. But if by making the industry subject to "economic planning" we merely mean that the responsibility of the works' managers is changed from the Iron and Steel Federation, or even the representatives of small groups of shareholders in competing firms, to a Public Corporation, responsible in its turn to a Supreme Economic Authority representing the people, then none of Professor Hayek's evils will fall upon us, and indeed the liberty of the employed person (representing four-fifths of the working population) is increased, in the only way it can be increased within the legal framework of an orderly democratic society, by the fact that he shares in making the laws and regulations under which he is required to work. [1]

6 Professor Hayek's strongest line of argument would be to show (as Professor Mises tried to show before him) that planning in my sense must lead to planning in his. But there is little evidence in the present book to suggest that Professor Hayek is now prepared to defend this proposition. Professor Mises used to say that centralising economic administration must lead to arbitrary budgeting, because any "interferences" with the pricing system would lead to confusion and make arbitrary decisions inevitable or, to put the same point in another way, that as planning was extended the logical *possibility* of using an automatic system of prices and costs would disappear. Little

---

[1]Professor Hayek is guilty of a strange inconsistency about personal liberty. The absence of it, in the political sphere, appals him. The absence of it, in the economic sphere, leaves him quite unmoved. On p. 19 he provides us with an eloquent definition:

"To the great apostles of political freedom the word has meant freedom from the arbitrary power of other men, release from the ties which left the individual no choice but obedience to the orders of a superior to whom he was attached."

It never seems to occur to him that *economic liberty* means exactly the same thing, and that one man employed by another, or by a large Corporation, is denied exactly the freedom in his economic relations that Professor Hayek wishes to preserve for him in his political life. The employed man is subject to coercion (of an economic kind), is given over to the "arbitrary [economic] power of other men", and "is left with no choice but obedience to the orders of an [economic] superior to whom he is attached"—particularly in a period of general unemployment. Nor is there any problem about discipline. Professor Hayek is perfectly aware that political liberty does not mean the absence of political authority and laws. We are politically free because we share in forming the laws, not because we can do what we like. If we are to become economically free, the same principle must apply—that we share in making the economic rules and determine the economic methods by which we are controlled. The social government of industry represents an expansion, and not a contraction, of the liberty in which we live.

trace of this familiar argument is to be found in Professor Hayek's present book—no doubt for the very good reason that it can no longer be sustained. The theory of value and economic accountancy has been generalised to such a degree that it applies as much, or as little, to a centrally directed economic system as to any other.

Instead of Professor Mises' incorrect but logical argument, we are now offered the most dubious kind of psychological and political dogmatism by Professor Hayek. The nearest approach to a statement of any reason why the centralising of administration should lead to dictatorial budgeting is contained in the mysterious passage to which I have already called attention—in which Professor Hayek says:

> "It may have been the unanimously expressed will of the people that Parliament should prepare a comprehensive economic plan, yet neither the people nor its representatives need therefore be able to agree on any particular plan. The inability of democratic assemblies to carry out what seems to be a clear mandate of the people will inevitably cause dissatisfaction with democratic institutions. . . . The conviction grows that if efficient planning is to be done the direction must be taken out of politics and placed in the hands of the experts" (p. 46).

Yet here the confusion over the meaning of "planning" completely obscures the issue. There will be no "unanimously expressed wish of the people . . . to prepare a comprehensive plan". There will be no "comprehensive plan"—but merely a change in the direction of economic responsibility, and Professor Hayek advances no reasons whatever for supposing that the new method will be less efficient than the old, or that the Central Planning Authority will not be able to use prices and costs to determine relative outputs, or need depart from the principle that consumers' preferences should guide production, or need limit the free choice of occupation.

Such arguments may exist, but they do not appear in this book, and all Professor Hayek's nightmares fade away in the cooler light of clearer definitions. There need be no arbitrary budgets, no dictation of occupation or consumption, no concentration camps or torture chambers, no frenzied gangsters in control, no night of freedom, no road to serfdom.

7 I now come to the *second* of my main criticisms of Professor Hayek's doctrine. Professor Hayek, although he does not

realise it, is really opposed to using reason and science in social affairs at all. The point may seem remote and philosophical but it is worth making. This is what Professor Hayek says:

> "Those who argue that we have to an astounding degree learned to master the forces of nature but are sadly behind in making successful use of the possibilities of social collaboration are quite right as far as this statement goes. But they are mistaken when they carry the comparison further and argue that we must learn to master the forces of society in the same manner in which we have learnt to master the forces of nature. This is not only the path to totalitarianism, but the path to the destruction of our civilisation and a certain way to block future progress. Those who demand it show by their very demands that they have not yet comprehended the extent to which the mere preservation of what we have so far achieved depends on the co-ordination of individual efforts by impersonal forces" (p. 152).

If the "mastery of social forces" could be secured only by the imposition of a dictatorial and comprehensive plan, Professor Hayek would be right. But if we contrast the principle of "free enterprise" as defined by him with the principle of "economic planning" as all democratic Socialists now describe it, then he is plainly wrong.

Both these principles are concerned with the administration of the scarce means of production. The difference between them is the presence or absence of conscious reason in the use of them. Professor Hayek rejects reason. We accept it.

Let me explain what I mean. Freedom of enterprise can be defended as something desirable only if it leads to stable and perfect competition, since, should the owners of property use their legal freedom to establish monopolies or monopolistic competition, the social good would be damnified and not served. Now, the essential condition of competitive production is that producers must remain blind to the real consequences of their actions and be governed purely by instinctive responses to external stimuli. The competitive entrepreneur is defined as a person controlling too small a fraction of the output of the commodity to influence its market price, or therefore to be aware of the true relations between the quantity of output, and the price of the commodity on the one hand, and the prices of the factors of production on the other. He is called upon to operate, unconsciously and blindly, the economic system that, collectively, he controls. "His not to reason why . . ." The principle of administration upon which society must therefore depend is nothing but a pattern of "conditioned reflexes"— automatic, unseeing, unreasoned—closely approximating to the way of life that governs communities of ants and bees. Men are condemned by Professor Hayek to remain for ever, in their economic affairs, in a pre-rational and pre-scientific age. They must allow their economic life to be directed by "impersonal forces" (created by themselves) that no person responsible for economic decisions can understand or direct. They must suffer unemployment and depressions and the persistence of excess capacity (all directly traceable to the inability of econo-mic administrators to foresee the results of their collective actions), just as their forefathers endured plagues and famine before the development of the sciences of medicine and agricul-ture gave us power to understand and thus to control the spread of human disease and the vagaries of the harvest.

The administrative principle of economic planning means necessarily the opposite of all this, and its successful practice would remove unnecessary ignorance as a source of poverty and economic frustration. The centralising of responsibility and the survey of economic resources as a whole enable the true pattern of cause and effect, and the real consequences of action, to be discovered. I do not mean by this that all economic problems will automatically be solved by, and all economic diseases immediately cured within, a planned economy. Far from it. The science of medicine has not yet cured all physical diseases, nor will it for many years to come. It is certain that great mistakes will be made in experimenting with new institutions. They always are. But Professor Hayek denies us the *possibility* of making the experiment, of using reason and foresight in the government of our economic affairs. We are never to direct these means to our chosen ends. Instead he fetters the primitive blindness of the conditioned reflex upon us in perpetuity and hands us over, tied hand and foot, to the unlighted anarchy of forces that he places for ever beyond our control. Human beings are not likely to tolerate such defeatism now—least of all democrats. They have learned to control their own political destiny. Why should they not master their economic fate?

Professor Hayek provides no good reason why they should not —because, as we have seen, he fails to distinguish centralised administration from authoritative budgeting. And I think he has been led to do this because he has confused means with ends at this deeper level. Professor Hayek might be right if he had argued that science cannot operate in the world of ends—although even there it is probable that observation, reason and comparison will throw much light upon the origin and nature of our moral judgments and moral conflicts. But even if this happens, it will still remain true that there is a sense in which moral and æsthetic values exist separately from reason and possess a sovereignty of their own. Thinking is not judging, and science cannot tell us what ends we should seek, what clothes we should wear, what food we should eat, or what pictures we should like, or whom we should love. It cannot, in short, decide for us what lives we ought to live. Observation and reason can illuminate, but they cannot replace, the activity of judgment and choice. The world of ends cannot be found by thought alone.

But this is not what the application of science to *economic* affairs entails. Professor Hayek, and those who think with him, are never tired of telling us that economics is a branch of study that deals with the law of *means*—not of ends. The same is true of the principles by which economic resources are administered —they are concerned with means, and not with ends. The institution of centralised responsibility can be made to serve any set of chosen ends and to organise any pattern of production and consumption whatever—just as much as the institution of free enterprise. But planning is likely to be a more efficient method of reaching any chosen set of ends because reason is superior to instinct and knowledge to ignorance, and Professor Hayek must admit as much unless, indeed, he calls upon us to reject in despair the opportunities and responsibilities of full humanity. He can drive science out of economic life only by preferring instinct to reason and ignorance to knowledge.

8 We are now left, in the *third* and last place, with Professor Hayek's historical arguments: that ". . . personal and political freedom has never existed in the past . . . without freedom in economic affairs" (p. 10), and the sad argument of his introduction that we are travelling by the German road, through economic planning to political slavery. These contentions lie somewhat outside the normal field of economic dis-

cussion, but it is scarcely possible to conclude this article without referring to them briefly.

The first of these arguments will scarcely bear examination. It is a plain case of *post hoc propter hoc*. It would be as sensible to say that political liberty has never existed without railways, and that therefore any growth of road transport was steadily undermining the spiritual sources of freedom. No one disputes the historical fact that during the seventeenth and eighteenth centuries there was a great movement of the social will that swept away the medieval and irrational limitations upon economic enterprise, and at the same time enlarged the popular basis of political sovereignty—at least, in this country. But this coincidence in time establishes no sequence of cause and effect. It is, indeed, more reasonable to take the view that the acquisition of power by the middle classes in the Reform Act of 1832 (Professor Hayek will remember that this Act enfranchised less than half a million persons on a high property qualification) was used by them to secure the kind of economic emancipation that, as a class, they most desired; and that the subsequent inclusion of the whole adult population in the councils of the nation is bringing to birth, in our day, the kind of economic *liberty* that we can all enjoy. It is most probable, in my view, that freedom of enterprise and the growth of responsible government were parallel consequences of an underlying, and slowly maturing, emotional emancipation that enabled the people of Britain to break the shackles of arbitrary authority in two directions at once, and which is now, in fuller strength and self-confidence, making us the masters of our economic as well as our political life. But whatever the true historical relation may be, it is quite impossible to argue that because free enterprise and political liberty grew up together they must disappear together.

This brings me to the second of Professor Hayek's historical arguments: that we are following the German road. This is what Professor Hayek says:

> ". . . Thus by moving from one country to another, one may sometimes twice watch similar phases of intellectual development. . . .
> When one hears for a second time of ideas expressed or measures advocated which one has first met twenty or twenty-five years ago, they assume a new meaning as symptoms of a definite trend. They suggest,

if not the necessity, at least the probability, that developments will take a similar course.

"*It is necessary now to state the unpalatable truth that it is Germany whose fate we are in some danger of repeating*" (p. 1).

". . . students of the currents of ideas can hardly fail to see that there is more than a superficial similarity between the kind of thought in Germany during and after the last war and the present current of ideas in this country. There is the same contempt for nineteenth-century liberalism, the same specious 'realism' and even cynicism, the same fatalistic acceptance of 'inevitable trends'. . . . All those whose memory goes further back know how deeply for at least a generation before the last war, German thought and German practice influenced ideals and policy in this country" (p. 2).

In short, Professor Hayek thinks that we are following the German road to slavery by an unconscious imitation of German thought. I have stated Professor Hayek's argument at length because it has always seemed strange to me that men and women coming to this island from the unhappy countries of Central Europe in which, through no fault of theirs, the practice of democracy has first been parodied and then trampled down, should not say to themselves, as they come among us, "Here is a people that have had no civil war for nearly three hundred years, who have led Europe in the ever-changing search for liberty, who have practised tolerance and kindliness before we were born—here they must have mastered some secret that is still hidden from us." But this never happens. Almost without exception we find that these visitors, welcome visitors, from abroad all feel sure that we are on the wrong road and moving towards the disasters with which they are only too familiar. The Communists tell us that we are in danger of a "Fascist dictatorship"; the men of the Right that we are a prey to Communism. Professor Hayek that we blindly follow the discredited teaching of nineteenth-century German professors into the abyss.

But surely the lesson of the historical comparison is exactly the opposite of the one that Professor Hayek seeks to draw. It shows that "ideas"—in the sense of political doctrines and social policies—are not the sole, nor perhaps the chief, causes of historical development and the formation of national character. The Germans in 1918 adopted the "ideas" of their conquerors. They accepted the doctrines of democracy. They wrote out paper constitutions. They attempted to play the democratic game. But the spirit was not there. The necessary virtue (particularly of tolerance and self-restraint) was not in them. The parody shuffled off the stage as soon as a depression undermined the weak confidence of the actors, and Hitler awoke the historical faith of the German people in military empire. The explanation of these matters lies deeper than Professor Hayek has yet looked—and we must call other studies to our aid before we can hope to understand them.

But if Professor Hayek sets store by these amateur historical interpretations, let him consider the experience of this country in my own lifetime. No one can dispute two facts: first, that in the last forty years we have departed widely from the practice of "free enterprise" as Professor Hayek would define it; and secondly, that political democracy has grown and flourished in the same period. The electorate has been more than doubled. The educational ladder has been lengthened and widened. Freedom of thought and speech has grown without halt. The Communist and Fascist Parties—the open enemies of democracy—have made less headway here than in any other European country. Our faith in the ancient institution of Parliament has not weakened. If Professor Hayek takes any account of the plainest facts of recent British experience he will find little support for his gloomy prophecies of catastrophe.

It therefore follows that, in this country, we have no need to fear the development of a centralised administration. We have a long tradition of increasing democracy combined with the growing activity of the State. For generations we have led the peoples of Europe in the art of self-government. We imitate no one, and it would be a thousand pities if Professor Hayek's false historical parallel should lead any of us to doubt our power to combine freedom with security and science with flexibility in the conduct of our economic affairs. If we have "economic planning" it will be our own "economic planning". It will fulfil the wishes of our people. It will be the servant of our freedom and will bring another part of our common life within the control of our social wisdom.

GOVERNMENT ADMINISTRATION AND EFFICIENCY[1]

Economic Planning means a great increase in the activity of the State. So does the extension of the Social Services and the all-embracing nature of modern military defence. For all these reasons it is most important that our machinery of Government administration should be continuously improved and that Civil Servants should be the best that we can get. It is therefore relevant to the purpose of this book to consider in what ways we fall short of the highest attainable standards. After five years' experience in the Civil Service I recorded my own conclusions on these matters.

A LARGE number of civilians drawn from the business community and from the academic profession have been recruited during the war to the Administrative Grade of the Civil Service. Many of them, including the present writer, have been disturbed by their experiences and feel impelled to make a number of criticisms and suggestions. The criticisms are not offered in a mood of complacent superiority. No profession is without its faults, and I am perfectly certain that Civil Servants brought, temporarily, into the ranks of my own profession (that of University teaching) would suffer the same disillusionment and comment with equal pertinence upon the besetting sins of dons—but I write in the confident belief that the suggestions for the reform of the Universities that Civil Servants could make, and would feel compelled to offer, at the end of three years, would be worth the most serious consideration of well intentioned University reformers. No profession is without fault or can wisely ignore the advice of candid friends.

1 Some criticism of the Civil Service and of the efficiency of Government Departments has, however, been ill-mannered

[1] Two articles in this series appeared in *The Political Quarterly*, January-March, 1944.

and intemperate, and it is necessary to begin by repudiating it, and insisting upon preserving some sense of proportion. A great deal of inefficiency and downright confusion was inevitable in the transition from peace to war, in the rapid multiplication of Government Departments, and in the expansion of the Service. Efficiency is normally the fruit of long labour and careful selection and can only be practised by a balanced team. It cannot be created overnight or practised by a rabble. A crowd, hastily assembled, is not an army.

Moreover, the Administrative Grade of the permanent Civil Service is characterised by four outstanding and positive virtues. The general level of intelligence is remarkably high (as a result of the standards imposed by the Entrance Examination) and compares favourably, in my view, with the average level reached in the two other professions that I know well—the academic and the political. Secondly, the co-operativeness of Civil Servants is, contrary to popular impressions, unusually great when they are left to themselves. Their humility (in the good sense) and their willingness to subordinate their personal interests to those of Departments of State is saintly in comparison with the vanity and self-seeking exhibited by dons and politicians.[1] Thirdly, they are very industrious and work long hours—too long in my view—and take few—too few—holidays. They are conscientious in a high degree. Finally they are financially incorruptible, eager to avoid any favouritism between the political Parties, or commercial interest, and they are, for the most part, loyal to their Ministers.

It is scarcely open to question that these clever, devoted and honest men, still provide this country with the best Civil Service in the world. If this is not so, what State is better served?

It is against the background of these virtues that all my subsequent criticisms must be judged. It would be dangerous to embark lightly upon the reform of a system that had produced and maintained these fundamental advantages—without which all other virtues would be worthless.

2 If our Civil Servants are intelligent, co-operative and incorruptible, what can be wrong with them?

[1]The humility they practise is "compensated" for, in the psychological sense, by a traditional and unreasonable contempt for, and hatred of, politicians—feelings that are carefully and successfully hidden from their objects!

There are, I think, five criticisms that can be justly made:

In the *first* place the administrative capacity of the Permanent Secretaries and Deputy Secretaries that I have met has been, with one or two notable exceptions, remarkably low. Perhaps I have been unfortunate in those whom I have known, but it has proved necessary to remove some of them as the war has proceeded, and it is impossible to escape the conclusion that most of them do not possess the gifts that one could reasonably expect of the fifty most important administrative officials in the country. They are intelligent, charming (for the most part) and conscientious men, but they are not men of imagination or action. They are slow, cautious and obstructive. They are "shrewd" but not wise, dependable but not creative. They are, too often, cynical rather than realistic. They are small men.

Of course, the job is not easy. Senior Civil Servants must be adaptable as well as constructive—for they must serve, with equal loyalty, successive Ministers from different Parties, with different policies, and of diverse temperaments. They must be able to calm an impatient Minister, press a lazy one and shield an incompetent. Nevertheless I cannot believe that the system of promotion has worked well. There must be fifty men who combine vigour with tact, imagination with efficiency, courage with realism, in a carefully selected Service drawn from the best men the Universities can provide. The truth of this view is strongly supported by the fact that there are such men to be found in the younger age groups within the Service. But they are not discovered and promoted in time.

In the *second* place the average level of personal vitality in the lower ranks of the Administrative Grade is not high—except in the Treasury. No doubt the younger and junior men take their colour from the Heads of their Departments, but, in addition to this, it is difficult to escape the conclusion that something has gone wrong with the method of recruitment. The young men (I have not met enough young women to generalise) admitted to the Service are clever and pleasant, but again with many notable exceptions, they are slightly prim young men, a shade stiff. They are not bouncing with vitality in the way that a group of young scientists, or young socialists, or young doctors, appear to be. It is difficult to imagine them raising their voices or hammering the table or denouncing the middle aged—giving way to the harmless vices of exuberance and youthful energy. One gets the impression that few Civil Servants, over the age of thirty, get out of bed in the morning feeling that anything of importance will have happened or could happen as a result of their own activity during the hours that must elapse before they get into it (the bed) again. This lack of conviction may be largely due to "the system", but it is not wholly due to it. It is partly due to the temperament of the selected men.

It may be that there is a tendency for young men of this kind to offer themselves for the Service just because it is safe. But an efficient method of selection would prevent too large a number of them getting in. No apparatus of written examinations or interviews is efficient if it fails to do this.

In the *third* place Civil Servants are characterised, again with marked exceptions, by a certain amateurishness and intellectual isolation. This weakness is particularly emphasized by the older permanent Civil Servants who have noticed a sharp decline during their lifetime in the amount of specialised and technical knowledge thought to be necessary or desirable by their younger colleagues. Certainly most Civil Servants exhibit an ignorance of the natural sciences and social studies related closely to their work that is very surprising to the outsider. It is impossible to justify this divorce of modern knowledge from the formation of policy. [1]

In the *fourth* place there is no systematic training provided for the young Assistant Principal on entering his career. In many cases the unfortunate young man spends two, three or four years—the formative years—sitting at his desk, sometimes in the same room as his superior, reading papers and supplying the first drafts of letters and documents for whose final form he bears no responsibility. The excessive formality, meticulous-

---

[1] The strangest example of this separation that has come within my personal experience is the ignorance of the rudiments of general economic and monetary theory exhibited by officials in the Treasury. There is considerable knowledge of the problems of the foreign exchange market and of taxation and budgetary economy—but little else. In no field did the separation between academic study and the formation of policy have more disastrous consequences in the years before the war. Fortunately, since the war began, Lord Keynes and other economists have been in a position to remedy this defect, and, as a consequence, this war has been incomparably better financed than the last.

ness and "paper-mindedness" of the older Civil Servant is to be traced more to this dreary initiation than to any other single cause. [1]

In the *fifth* place the work of the Establishment Divisions—the Divisions concerned with staffing organisation—is poor. This is partly due to the tradition of short-sighted "economy" that has prevented the modernisation and proper equipment of Government offices—a point to which I shall return in a moment. But the weakness of the Establishment Division is also due to the poor calibre of the officers who take up work in the Establishment Divisions. It has become traditional in many Departments to send men who are not much good for anything else into this Division—it has become a retiring ground for the mediocre and the "misfits". It is, therefore, a "blind alley" occupation, and few men passing into it can entertain any hope of reaching the highest offices in the Service. Yet upon the work of this Division depends the efficiency of the whole office—as an office. The essential skeleton of the mechanism is in their hands, and it is not surprising that the machine should be inefficient if its designers are second-rate.

3 It is, I think, commonly agreed that, in all these listed respects, the position has deteriorated between the two wars. It is interesting to speculate on the reason for the decline. In the minds of most observers it cannot be separated from, and may indeed be wholly due to, the similar and greater decline in the calibre of Cabinet Ministers—with the causes of which these Notes are not concerned. But it is in the highest degree probable that more vigorous and imaginative Ministers would have selected, over a period of years, Civil Servants who were men of action and who would have communicated their leadership and "drive" through the hierarchy of the Service. In addition it is said that the increasing influence of the Treasury in the nomination of men for the highest posts has been detri-

---

[1] In certain Departments a serious attempt has been made to provide an adequate training for the young recruits, and it is becoming increasingly common to send them "out into the field"—to a Colony, or a Post Office, or a Labour Exchange. This is the most important form of training if the administrator is to understand the living reality of the thing administered, and the practice should be generalised and systematised. In addition, however, it is also desirable that the young Civil Servant should learn something of the methods of administration practised by private Corporations and should also be given an opportunity to study the subjects that are of especial relevance to the work of his Department.

mental to efficiency in two ways; first that it has made the senior Civil Servants, naturally eager for promotion, too sensitive to the opinion, and too eager to secure the good will of the Treasury; and secondly that in recent years a tendency has appeared for the Head of the Treasury to use his influence to select men of flexible mind, who have received a more general training as Private Secretaries to Ministers instead of the older type of Departmental specialists. Whatever the cause of the disease may be—it is essential to find a cure.

4 What can be done to improve the efficiency of the Service? No single remedy for these weaknesses exists, and it is, in any case, highly probable that the efficiency of the Government machine cannot be substantially improved unless and until the average ability of Cabinet Ministers (in peace-time) has been considerably increased.[1] They are, after all, the real "Heads of the Department", and Civil Servants are servants— and must remain so. No school can remain good under a series of bad headmasters, and no Department of State can, in practice, remain administratively "fit" under a succession of vague, short-sighted, inactive political Chiefs. Reform, to be completely effective, must extend to the top.

With this problem I am not concerned. Whether we are to have good or bad Ministers we shall always need a Civil Service, and it will continue to make an essential contribution to the complex process of democratic government; and there is, therefore, every reason for improving the efficiency of the persons in it.

The Service could be improved in three ways—by better methods of recruitment, by better methods of training, by better methods of promotion. Any team of men, assembled for any purpose, could be improved by drafting better people into it, or giving them better instruction when they are in it, or perfecting the methods by which the Captain is chosen. In

[1]There is a natural and inevitable improvement in the calibre of Ministers in the war. In the first place all the main Parties are represented in the Government, and it is therefore easy to form Ministries of the "best men willing to serve". In the second place it is possible during war to overcome the Trade Unionism of the professional politician and to bring in able men from outside. In the third place we are a little more ruthless during time of war and do get rid of a large number of men who have proved incompetent—adjusting a little the balance between seniority and ability in favour of ability. As a consequence we secured by the third year of each of these wars a very able team of Ministers, and our remarkable triumphs of organisation are directly traceable to this fact.

addition there is the special problem of status, or tenure of the highest offices, to be considered. I propose to touch upon each of these problems in turn.

5 Recruitment. There are two ways in which it would be possible, in my view, to improve the methods of selection.

(*a*) The normal method of entry at the age of twenty-one or two should, needless to say, remain open and competitive—but the kind of tests that are used should be modernised.

The present written examination has served an invaluable purpose. It has kept the Civil Service intelligent. But intelligence is not enough, and the written examination needs to be supplemented (not replaced) by something better than the present "interview". The interview in the Examination for the Administrative Grade, to which nearly a quarter of the total marks has been accorded in recent years, is a poor affair. An oddly selected Committee of persons (including titled ladies) whose claim to deep psychological insight is far from obvious, are asked to sit hour after hour, day after day (for as long as six weeks) "interviewing" candidates for periods ranging from ten to fifteen minutes. Such a procedure approximates to a farce. Anyone who has had any experience in interviewing candidates for any post or scholarship will realise that a bored and exhausted Committee, however fair and conscientious, can arrive at nothing but the crudest "hit and miss" judgments after a few minutes conversation with candidates who are strained and anxious.

Plainly this miserable arrangement can be improved upon, and the present interview should be replaced by a modern combination of intelligence tests, practical tests and psychiatrical examinations such as those used by the more progressive business houses and in the "pre-OCTU" Selection Boards now set up for the Army. Anyone who doubts the value of these more scientific methods of selection should study the procedure and results, as measured by "follow-up" statistics, of these Boards.

I do not suggest that any new kind of test should wholly replace, at any rate for a time, the older written Examination—of whose virtues we are at least sure. But since no one proposes that we should put the clock back thirty years and dispense with the "interview" altogether, we should at least make the "non-written" test as good and as scientific as possible; and when confidence in the justice and validity of the new method of judgment is firmly established the relative importance of the practical and psychiatrical tests might be weighed equally with the written papers.

And I feel convinced that the improvement of the interview would do something to adjust the balance between intelligence and vitality more wisely. The present written Examination picks out the intelligent, but a Committee of bored amateurs, talking to an endless stream of candidates for ten minutes apiece, places an undue premium upon pleasant manners, quiet modesty and friendliness, and charges too heavy a discount against "pushfulness", "bumptiousness" and "toughness". A better form of "interview" would diminish the prejudice in favour of "charm" and against "vitality".

(b) I think it is a mistake to suppose that recruitment to the Civil Service should take place exclusively at the age of twenty-two or twenty-three. The Service needs a variety of experience, and there is no reason why it should be deprived completely of the services of men who have proved themselves to be good at administration. Few men can have done that at the age of twenty-two. There is no reason, however, why a small number of posts at a senior level (say one quarter of the posts held by Assistant Secretaries) should not be filled by men in their early thirties drawn from outside the Service by advertisement and open competition.

It would be essential to avoid any suggestion of political "colour" in the making of these appointments. We have set our faces steadily, and probably wisely, in this country against anything that savours of the "spoils" system. But nothing of the kind is implied by this proposal. The appointments should be made by the reformed Civil Service Commission (whose constitution I shall briefly describe in a later paragraph), they would be advertised and open to all comers (including permanent members of the Service), and impartial methods of selection would be exclusively employed. Hence no suspicion of political influence need arise, while the advantages of such a practice would be considerable. The inflow of men at a later stage in life, and at a higher level, would continually freshen the Service, keep it in touch with the development of administrative technique, maintain its intellectual communication with the larger world, and do a great deal to break down the cloistered separateness of Whitehall—the "place apart".

6 Training. Once the young man (or young woman) has been selected, he or she needs, like anyone else, a special vocational training. This should be provided in two stages:

(a) The young recruit or Assistant Principal should in all cases, and not merely in some, be sent out into the field. He should spend his first year touring various sections of his Department in Whitehall, in the Registry, in the Establishment Division, in a policy Division; but then he should be moved for a substantial period into the sector of human life he is proposing to administer—an Assistant Principal in the Board of Education should spend six months in the schools and offices of a Local Education Authority; an Assistant Principal in the Board of Trade should spend six months or a year in a factory or a commodity market; an Assistant Principal in the Ministry of Transport should work, not only in the Regional Offices of the Ministry, but also upon a railway and in the office of a bus company and a Road Authority. In every branch of administration the individual admitted at the top should begin all over again at the bottom. He must see his Department from outside, work below the harrow as well as above it, widen his experience, and live in a world peopled by men and women, rather than papers and files walking.

It is also most important that very early in his career he should be entrusted with some field, however small, of personal responsibility. The paralysing influence of constant supervising and complete subordination must be removed. It does not matter how small and unimportant the job may be—if it only consists in organising the messenger Service or providing drawing pins to Local Education Authorities— as long as he finds himself in a position in which he must take decisions and subsequently defend them without relying upon the authority of his superiors, becoming responsible for a little world in which something happens as a result of his labours. There is no other way of avoiding the slow growth of cynicism, the consequence of an unacknowledged sense of futility, that saps the administrative vitality of far too many Civil Servants before they have reached the age of forty.

(*b*) It is now commonly agreed, I believe, that at a later age, after some ten years in the Service, in the early thirties, the Civil Servant should be given the opportunity, and indeed required, to enjoy a further period of vocational study and training. This is the essence of the idea behind the present agitation for a Civil Service Staff College.

The opponents of change will no doubt make some obstructive use of his choice of a name by arguing that the requirements of military training are quite different from those of civil "administration"; and that it is impossible to teach "administrators" anything because there is no agreed "science of administration". All this is quite beside the point. It is true that it would be unwise to press the analogy between the new proposals and the existing Military Staff Colleges too far— but the absence of any strict parallelism between them does not weaken the case for two positive provisions in the case of the Civil Service.

In the first place nothing but good could come from releasing men for a "sabbatical year" between the ages of thirty and thirty-five to renew their academic studies and to travel. It does all specialists good to escape for a breathing space from the professional prison that closes around all but the best of us as soon as the years of intellectual maturity have been reached. To move in a larger world, to meet men and women with different backgrounds, and to "see how the other half lives" does us all good. Dons have benefited enormously from their short life as Civil Servants, and what is sauce for the goose is sauce for the gander.

I would not wish, myself, to put any exclusive emphasis upon the element of "holiday" in the sabbatical year. It should be a period of serious study and intellectual development, and it should, in my opinion, have a strong vocational flavour. Officials released from the Board of Trade should not spend the whole year in reading modern poetry but should spend some of their time in studying recent theories of foreign trade or industrial organisation at the London School of Economics or observing, in the United States of America, the work of the Federal Trade Commission, or working in the office of a large

Corporation. The official from the Colonial Office should attend lectures in anthropology and study, in the field, the campaigns for mass adult education conducted in Russia. In all cases it would be desirable to combine a course of study in the most important relevant fields of scientific research with travel and the investigation of some practical administrative achievement in another country. Intellectual and geographical isolation must both be destroyed.

In the second place I believe (though this second idea might not gain such wide support) that no harm could be done by introducing a second general test, at this higher age. Few of us are so good that we can dispense with a periodical stimulus to gather all our forces together and do our best to jump over another hurdle. There is therefore every reason why the studies of the "sabbatical year" should end with some sort of assessment, made by the Civil Service Commissioners and corresponding to the "passing out" examination of a Service Staff College, in which the candidates were awarded classes that would be considered whenever the question of their future promotion was raised. Nor is there any reason why the more modern methods of judging a man, to which I have already referred, should not also be used at this stage in the career of the Civil Servant—or of any profession for that matter.

7 One problem of training deserves a further word. I have already pointed out that the work of, and the capacity of the men serving in, most Establishment Divisions, is very poor; and there is every reason why the status of this specialised profession within the Service should be raised and a suitable training provided for it. There may be no agreed "science of administration" in the sense that it would prove of equal value to the Permanent Under-Secretary of the Foreign Office and a Principal in the Ministry of Health—but there can surely be no question that there is an immense amount that can now be taught, and learned, about the business of organising an office efficiently. The existing courses in "Business Administration", including the subjects of recording, planning, accounting, personnel management and the rest, undoubtedly contain a large body of information that is of great relevance to the work of any Establishment Division. It would therefore be desirable, in my view, to make it a rule that men and women intending to specialise in this field should spend part of their "sabbatical leave" in Courses and Colleges primarily concerned with the study of these matters.

8 Promotion. Selection and promotion within the Service could be improved, in my view, by making two changes.

(*a*) It is commonly agreed that it is an error to unite the duties of accounting and economy with that of advising on promotion to the highest posts in one Department. As one business man has justly said:

"If we had allowed our Accountants to get the whip-hand—to determine the policy of, and select the Heads for, all our other Departments—we should have been bankrupted long ago."

It is wrong that the Treasury should, at one and the same time, discharge the honourable and essential duty of "watchdog" in the interests of the taxpayer, and exert an important influence in choosing Secretaries and Deputy Secretaries for every other Government Department. Acceptability to the Treasury is not the primary virtue in the Head of any Office.

On the other hand, it would be undesirable to leave the selection of Secretaries wholly in the hands of the Minister of the day; and to lose the opportunity of moving men from Department to Department and thus preserving a rough equality of personal efficiency at the various levels of the Service. And the Head of the Treasury is in a better position than anyone else to judge the relative competence of the Senior Civil Servants since he personally sees most of them at work.

The solution of this dilemma is not far to seek—the duty of supervising promotion should be taken from the Treasury and placed in the hands of an enlarged and reformed Civil Service Commission. The new Commissioners would then be charged with four tasks—recruiting the Service, ensuring the proper training of all Assistant Principals, running the "Staff College" and supervising promotion throughout the Administrative Grade. They would become a "Personnel Department" for the whole apparatus of government.

Promotion to the Headships of Departments would remain in the hands of the Prime Minister (acting in consultation with the Minister of the day), and he (the Prime Minister) would be advised by the Senior Commissioner after the Commissioner had consulted the Head of the Treasury, who would remain, for all other purposes, the Head of the Civil Service. Below this rank senior appointments would be made by the Departmental Minister, advised in his turn by the Commissioners after consultation with the Permanent Head of the Department. By this method it should prove possible to secure the advantages of Treasury control without suffering from the evil consequences of the present arrangement.

(*b*) No one wishes to introduce any form of, or approximation to, the "spoils system" in this country. One of the reasons for our greater administrative efficiency and deeper political stability is, no doubt, to be found in the fact that our Civil Servants are guaranteed security of tenure, that they do not change office with their political chiefs and are, in some measure, independent of them. This arrangement secures continuity in administration and makes it possible for Civil Servants to make regular careers in the Service and offer honest advice, if they are courageous men, to politicians.

But, as in many other walks of life, it is easy to have too much of a good thing, and we have gone on from offering Civil Servants continuity of employment to giving them security in particular posts. A man is not only guaranteed a salary and a job. He is also secure in the office he holds unless he is guilty of gross moral fault or negligence. In short, unsuitability for the work he has been called upon to do is no ground for dismissal. This unnecessary extension of a valid principle has two unwelcome consequences. In the first place a Minister is not sufficiently master in his own household. He carries the formal responsibility. He is answerable to Parliament for the conduct of his Department, and it is an unwritten, but unbreakable, convention of the Constitution that he should not lay the blame, in public, upon the Civil Servants to whom he has delegated his powers for any mistake that they may have made in using them. Yet he finds it unduly difficult to remove the most important "servants" who have failed him. If he has no confidence in his Permanent Secretary he must embark upon an elaborate, and usually indirect, intrigue to get rid of him. It is almost impossible, therefore, for a Minister to make sure he is well served, and this is a paradoxical and unnecessary limitation upon his power. In the second place too much security is no good to anyone. A Civil Servant can only go up. He can never go down. He has no immediate motive to keep himself administratively fit and creative. This is an unfortunate consequence, and undesirable form of "security". Can it be safely altered?

In my view it could. I believe that it would be possible to remove the security in particular posts without disturbing the independence of the Civil Servant or introducing the "spoils system". It should be made possible for a Minister (or a Permanent Secretary) to remove an Official from the position he occupies, on the ground that he is unsuitable for this particular post, without necessarily reflecting on his (or her) capacity for other duties. Such persons would remain at their substantive rank but come back to the care of the Civil Service Commissioners who would seek to place them elsewhere. In this way a new element of flexibility and a desirable incentive to efficiency could be introduced without losing the security of tenure that is essential and the independence of judgment that springs from it. The power of the Minister within his Department would approximate more closely to his formal responsibilities, and the small initial cost to the Treasury would be offset by the increased efficiency of the administrative machine.

9 So far as I have concentrated upon the weaknesses of, and the methods by which, the Civil Service might be improved. It may be worth adding a word or two about the work of the Departments. This is a vast subject, and the experience of any one temporary Civil Servant is very limited and makes an insufficient basis for many generalisations. Nevertheless, there

are certain criticisms that I have found to be very generally made by my fellow "temporaries".

Again it is necessary to stress the great differences between the Departments and the Divisions within them. Some are efficient. Some are not. Some work smoothly. Some are chaotic. But there are certain features of Government administration that force themselves upon the mind of a candid outsider. I shall mention four of them.

10 In the first place there is a marked failure to define and delegate spheres of responsibility. It is never easy to find anyone who is finally responsible for anything. Decisions must continually be referred to other people—either upwards to more important officials or outwards to other Departments. Files containing a single letter or an unimportant trifle, may have to pass through seven or eight hands before a reply can be made. I have frequently attended Committees on which fifty or sixty officials normally sat. This slowness and complexity, together with the temperamental willingness of the Civil Servant to avoid responsibility is what we all mean when we denounce "bureaucracy" and "red tape" and "Civil Service methods".

There are two immediate causes for this phenomenon—a minor and a major cause.

The "minor cause"—of which far too much has been made in the past—is the fact that the Minister and his Department are responsible to Parliament. A Member of Parliament may ask any question he pleases about the affairs of any Department of State and the Minister must reply in the House. Or he may write letters that must be answered with care. And the Permanent Head of the Department is responsible to the Public Accounts Committee and may be called upon to justify the smallest item of expenditure before it. For this reason excessively meticulous accounts and paper records must be kept.

There are many ways in which this evil could be mastered. Many Departments could create a better, swifter and more specialised machine for answering enquiries of all kinds. There is also no reason why a more realistic convention should not be adapted by Ministers answering questions in the House. They might frequently say, when it is true: "Yes, a mistake has been made. I am formally responsible for what has happened and

I have looked into the matter, and I can assure the House that the appropriate remedy has been applied and the same error will not recur. On the other hand it is impossible that a large organisation should not make many mistakes, and I am sure the House will not press the criticism too far or extend it too widely."

Finally, it is time that Parliament recognised that its machinery of supervision is out of date and ill suited to the complexity of modern government. More discretion should be allowed to Departmental Officials and Parliamentary enquiry should be limited to larger questions and the prevention of corruption.

But the major reason for complexity and delay is, however, more fundamental than the existence of responsibility to Parliament. The real impediment to action is the need for "co-ordination" and is a function of size. The larger the Department, the bigger the State, the more persons must be informed and consulted before a policy can develop consistently. Take an example. Suppose a small firm writes to the Ministry of Supply asking for a continuation of its contract to produce shell-caps or for a licence to extend its machine shop. The difficulty of coming to a decision is much greater than might, at first sight, appear. The Director of the Division responsible for making shell-caps must first pass upon the matter. He will want to know the opinion of his local representative about the record and efficiency of the firm. He must consult the Treasury on the cost of the extension and the proportion to be borne by the Treasury—otherwise money may be wasted or different firms may be offered quite different terms. He must consult the Ministry of Labour to discover whether labour is relatively scarce or relatively abundant in the area in which the firm is situated—otherwise there will be complete confusion (as there often has been) in the geographical distribution of work. He must consult the Ministry of Aircraft Production to make sure that they are not going to offer new contracts to this firm—otherwise there will be a disastrous competition between Government Departments. He must consult the lawyers of his own Ministry on the legal terms of the contract. Finally, he must obtain the sanction of his superior, and of the Planning Department of the Ministry of Supply, and perhaps, if he is especially meticulous, he will also have a word with the Ministry of Production, in order to make sure that this particular increment of shell-caps is consistent with the larger "production plans" of which this programme is a part. But all this "co-ordination" takes time and effort, and I have chosen a particularly simple case. Many decisions would require consultations with a dozen, rather than half a dozen, different persons and Departments before consistence was secured. All this is inevitable.

Now there are two methods by which this necessary "co-ordination" can be obtained—either an Inter-Departmental Committee can be appointed to plan a series of contracts for shell-caps, or a man can be given the responsibility to produce shell-caps and charged with the duty of securing proper "co-ordination" with'other Government Departments. There can be no doubt, in my view, that the second course is preferable to the first. "Co-ordination" is essential, but so is "drive" and independent action. The only way to complete any complex administrative task, and overcome the inertia of large institutions, is to place the responsibility plainly and firmly upon the shoulders of one man and give him the necessary powers so that he can either succeed or fail. If he fails, or if he cannot fit his plans into the complex pattern of Government policy, then he must go and someone else must tackle the job in his stead. There is no other method by which vigour can be combined with consultation, and action with democracy. The wider recognition and practice of this principle in Whitehall is fundamental to the achievement of higher levels of efficiency. Unfortunately the principle is not yet sufficiently recognised and a great deal of time and energy is wasted on inter-Departmental Committees that have no powers and no full-time officers to carry out their "decisions".

All other points are of secondary importance in comparison with this first matter—this is the heart of the administrative problem.

11 In the second place there is often a marked failure to communicate policy downwards. It is almost impossible for the officials in the lower ranks of the hierarchy (Principals and Assistant Secretaries) to discover what is happening, or what decisions have been taken, in the fields for which they are

responsible. I have met Assistant Secretaries more than once who remained in complete ignorance of Cabinet conclusions for weeks after they had been arrived at despite the fact that they were of immediate importance for their work. I even came across an Assistant Secretary (an experienced Civil Servant of many years standing) who had not heard that the subject for which he was responsible had been referred, by the Cabinet, to a Ministerial Committee four months before; and had never seen the papers submitted to, or the minutes arising from, their frequent meetings since that date. In neither of these cases did any difficulty arise on grounds of security—there was no special need for secrecy. Such cases are no doubt extreme. They have to be encountered to be believed, but they are symptomatic of the deep obscurity in which the policy of the Government is sometimes shrouded from those who have to implement it, and the absence of proper arrangements to make policy known throughout the Service. This deficiency explains some of the confusion and inconsistency in detail of which we all became aware in dealing with Government Departments. Policy is only intelligible at the top.

It would be easy to remedy these defects by introducing devices that are familiar outside Whitehall. The efficient system would differ from Department to Department. In some —the smaller ones no doubt—the "Departmental Meeting" is the natural solution. The Minister and the Permanent Secretary should meet all the officials above the rank of Principal at least once a week to communicate changes of policy to them and to discuss a Progress Report. If such meetings are needed in the life of academic institutions, in which the amount of administrative action is much less, they are far more essential to the smooth running of a large Government Department. In others it would be desirable to circulate a carefully prepared Progress Report or "House Journal" in which a more formal account of changes in policy and a record of action could be provided. Such a document would, of course, possess no value unless it were taken seriously and made the direct responsibility of a senior official—the Permanent Secretary or the Deputy Secretary—but it would prove invaluable if it were informed and properly edited. Finally, another attempt should be made to produce a readable and interesting "vocational journal" for the whole Administrative Grade of the Service—corresponding to the technical periodicals published for any other professions —doctors, lawyers or economists. Such journals have not proved successful in the past—but it is difficult to believe that a weekly publication produced under the auspices of the Treasury, containing confidential but not secret information, and including a review of new legislation, Orders in Council and Blue Books of general interest, and a section devoted to the scientific problems of government and administration, would not prove an indispensable piece of reading for the competent Civil Servant.

12 In the third place some of the staffing arrangement in Government Departments are most peculiar—they appear "top-heavy" to a newcomer. Too little clerical and secretarial aid is provided for administrative officers. This is an extravagant and inconvenient piece of "economy". Men and women, who are paid as much as £1,500 a year to do administrative work, are not given personal secretary-typists. They have to get their own telephone numbers, make their own appointments, provide themselves with typists out of the "typing pools", summon messengers and do all sorts of trivial jobs. A considerable part of their time—paid at the rate of £800— £1,500 a year—is spent on work that could and should be performed by girls glad to earn £150 a year. This means a considerable waste of money and a loss of administrative efficiency, to the Department as a whole. Two Principals with personal secretaries could do as much work as three Principals without secretaries, and do it better at a smaller cost. No doubt a good deal of "sharing" and "pooling" would be desirable, but the existing "pools" are far too big and do not provide the time-saving services that are required. The distribution of staff between grades should be radically overhauled.

13 Finally, it is necessary to call attention to the very low standards of the physical arrangements in Government Offices. These are surprisingly poor and depressing. The interiors of the buildings are old-fashioned, gloomy, dirty, and in some cases almost insanitary. The rooms in which all grades of the Civil Service are condemned to work, below the level of Assistant Secretary, are meanly furnished and arranged with the maximum of inconvenience. They are not modern office

buildings—for obvious historical reasons—but they have not been reconstructed behind the existing façades or adequately "improved". The physical environment in which the Civil Servant works is squalid and overcrowded. There is no room for comfort or quiet for thought. There are no proper reading rooms in the Libraries, no Common Rooms or (in peace-time) good Canteens or Restaurants. There is nothing to make anyone feel at home in a Government Office, or glad to get there in the morning, or anything but delighted to leave it at night. These conditions, trivial as they may seem, are not without their importance in preserving vigour and harmony among any team of busy men and women.

In addition to all this, and of more immediate importance, is the correspondingly low level of the services provided in the Offices. Perhaps my experiences were unfortunate and not typical, but in the first office to which I went—a new war-time Department—the standards were deplorably low. The typists from the "pool" could not type. The "shorthand-writers" could not write shorthand. The girls on the switch-board could not operate a telephone, and the switch-board was so over-loaded that it was often necessary to wait for three or four minutes before one could begin to make a call. There were four of us in one small room, using artificial light most of the day, and the atmosphere was one of chaotic pandemonium. These intolerable inconveniences between them wasted half one's time. And I have reason to believe that in many of the older Departments, even in peace-time, conditions are not markedly better.

The reasons for this congestion and physical inefficiency in Government Offices are not far to seek. They are partly due to the short-sighted parsimony of Parliament and the Treasury. As long as Parliament believes that wise economy in administration is secured by over-working and over-crowding its most important officials there cannot be much improvement in physical standards. The failure is further due to the poor performances of the Establishment Divisions to which I have already referred. Fortunately the methods of improvement are equally obvious. An extensive programme of new building, re-building, and reconstruction within existing buildings, together with an enlargement in the duties, and an improve-

ment in the selection and training of men and women for the
Establishment Divisions, would work wonders in a comparatively short space of time. These are the easy changes to bring
about.

14 To sum up. There is no reason to despair. We have
worked miracles in organising ourselves for war. This small
island, with its forty-five million inhabitants, aided by twenty
million white citizens within the borders of the Empire, has
armed itself with spectacular speed and has, in three years,
produced the most powerful navy, the finest fighter force, the
largest bomber fleets, and some of the best armies that the world
has ever seen. We are the smallest of the Great Powers, but
we are the most completely mobilised and the most productive.
This is a triumph of organisation. In the successful completion
of this immense task the Civil Service has played a vital and
honourable part. We are still the best governed and the best
administered modern state, and our Civil Service is the best
in the world.

But we cannot stay still or rest upon our laurels, however
green. After the war is over we shall have complex administrative problems to resolve. The sphere of Governmental
activity will be permanently increased. We must improve
(restore some would say) the efficiency of the Civil Service
and machinery of the State. By what methods can that be
done?

After some experience of academic and business administration, and over three years spent inside more than one Department of State, I offer the following positive suggestions:

First, the recruitment to the Civil Service should be improved
by introducing modern methods of selection into the preliminary interview; and by taking in a small proportion of older
men to higher posts.

Secondly, the training of the Assistant Principal should be
made systematic, should always include a period of work in the
field; and should be followed, between the ages of thirty and
thirty-five, by a further period of vocational training in scientific
and practical disciplines, and by a further examination.

Thirdly, promotion within the Service should be supervised
by a reformed and enlarged Civil Service Commission, and
Ministers and Permanent Secretaries should be able to remove

men and women from the posts they hold without dismissing them from the Service.

Fourthly, more responsibility should be devolved upon individuals and "co-ordination" (consistency in policy) should be secured by requiring these men to make the necessary consultations. Personal responsibility should not be confused and lost in a thicket of inter-Departmental Committees.

Fifthly, better arrangements should be made—including "Office Councils", internal "House journals", and an official Whitehall magazine—to communicate policy downwards and render it more intelligible to the lower levels of the official hierarchy.

Sixthly, the principles of staffing should be overhauled and physical conditions and secretarial services of the Offices should be greatly improved.

All these steps are separately desirable and, taken together, would secure a marked improvement in the efficiency of our system of Departmental Administration.

Paper VII

SOCIAL SIGNIFICANCE OF THE THEORY OF VALUE

*In the following article (published in the "Economic Journal" in 1935)
I tried to show why the institutions of competition do not, and in my
view cannot, lead to a wise direction of our economic life—or (putting
the same proposition into technical jargon) why the optimal distribution
of our resources, defined in the theory of value, does not result from
openistic competition. If this negative proposition is accepted the problem
of the next article then arises—how can the theory of value be applied
within the institutions of a planned economy.*

T HE purpose of this article is to examine the view that
the theory of value can be used to defend that particular
organisation of economic life which is based on the institutions of competition and of private property in the material
factors of production.

2 The theory of value is used in two quite different ways to
throw light upon the problem of economic organisation:

In the first place it is used to elucidate one important aspect
of that problem. It analyses the logical implications of a pre-
supposed scarcity of means necessary to the achievement of
certain ends. It reveals the existence of the problem of choice
and emphasises the importance of a trustworthy economic
calculus. It reveals the relationship between this calculus and
personal liberty in consumption. It shows that only one kind
of calculus will do, and that if individual consumers are to be
free to influence the relative outputs of commodities in order to
secure that combination of goods which they prefer, there is
one arrangement of resources which is better than any other.
Such an arrangement can only be revealed by discovering the
value of the marginal products of mobile resources in all uses. [1]

---

[1]It has frequently been argued that such a principle is invalid because (*a*)
a free pricing system may reduce total output, and (*b*) relative productivities
have no meaning in a regime of unequal incomes. Such arguments, however,

5*   127

But all these forms of the theory are purely analytic. They show the logical implications of certain assumptions. They diagnose the problem of combining a utilitarian calculus with liberty, but they tell us nothing of the institutions by which the real problem of arrangement can be solved.

In the second place, however, the traditional theory of value does go beyond mere diagnosis or formal logic. The theory of competition sets out to show that, under a certain set of actual legal institutions, the correct calculations and the best arrangement of resources (in the above sense) will be made. Reduced to its barest outline the theory of competitive equilibrium attempts to prove, (*a*) that if the goods demanded by the consumers can be subdivided so that there are many buyers and many units of demand, and (*b*) that if production can be organised without technical loss in a number of separate manufacturing and commercial units, the best arrangement of resources will be secured by private property in land and capital. [1]

The theoretical demonstration requires two further conditions that are not always stated plainly. The atomic producers must possess a peculiar *type of foresight*. They must have enough foresight to plan production so as to maximise their long-period profits. Otherwise they would fail to make the adjustments necessary to secure *the best* technical arrangements for production. But they must not possess too much foresight, or they may cease to compete. Again, competitive equilibrium will only be reached as long as the *rate of change in the data*—the underlying demand and cost functions—is not greater than the maximum

miss the essential point. In the first place, no convincing reasons have ever been advanced for supposing that a system of costing aimed at satisfying consumers' demands would reduce output. Why should one arrangement of resources be more difficult to achieve than another? In the second place, the principle is independent of the distribution of income. If income were equally distributed the ideal of freely chosen consumption remains. There may be something to say for bringing about the redistribution of income in a transitional stage partly by subsidising the goods consumed by the poor and taxing those consumed by the rich. But such a policy would leave the principle of consumers' freedom unaffected. The principles concerning the distribution of income are independent of the way in which the recipients of income can effect the distribution of resources. See Dickinson, *Economic Journal*, 1933; Maurice Dobb and A. Lerner, *Review of Economic Studies*, 1934, for discussions of this problem.

[1] See T. E. Gregory's *An Economist Looks at Planning*, passim; Hayek, "The Trend of Economic Thinking", *Economica*, 1933; Robbins, *The Great Depression*, Chaps. VII and VIII, passim, particularly Chap. VIII; Plant, *Journal of Transport*, 1933; and *Collectivist Economic Planning*, especially Hayek's "The Present State of the Debate".

Social Significance of the Theory of Value

speed of adjustment of which the producers are capable. Otherwise the competitive adjustment will always be towards a situation that has already become irrelevant and no tendency to equilibrium would be present.[1]

On the basis of these four assumptions it has frequently been claimed that the theory of value proves that private enterprise will secure the best arrangement of resources for any "want and production system" whatever.

The conclusion is held to follow wherever the conditions of scarcity exist, and to apply to any type of product whose use and manufacture can both be sufficiently subdivided. Each product will absorb just that quantity of mobile resources which is desirable.[2] Property in capital resources and the pursuit of private profit are sufficient incentives and imply sufficient wisdom to bring such an atomic world into equilibrium. It has even been demonstrated that the private ownership of relatively small plots of land will cause a railway line between two places to follow the "economically desirable" route despite the indivisibility of the line itself.[3] As the theory of value has been extended to cover more and more obscure cases in recent years, it is not unnatural that it has also been used as part of a rationale of the institutions of individual enterprise. But to prove that one set of institutions will achieve a desired end does not prove that no other set can achieve it better. A different set of arrangements and sanctions might very well achieve the same end more expeditiously and more justly than competition and private property. It has been argued that a planned socialism provides just this better way. But it is not with the problems of economic calculus in a planned economy that we are for the moment concerned; rather with the claims made on behalf of private property and competition.

3 It should be apparent at once that the theory of competitive equilibrium can cover only part of the economic field. Any end which cannot be atomised cannot be dealt with by an atomic analysis. Such ends are common. Satisfaction may be derived from the contemplation or enjoyment of a certain set of relations embracing all elements in an economy instead of from

[1]See Rosenstein-Rodin, *Economica*, 1934.
[2]See Marshall's *Principles*, Book V; Pigou, *Economics of Welfare*, Part II, etc.
[3]An unpublished paper by Mr. R. G. D. Allen.

129

the consumption of a physically divisible commodity like boots. The enjoyment of economic equality, for example, means the establishment of an indivisible set of relations between all the human factors of production in so far as they are recipients of final income. Security from disease demands the observance of certain rules and the performance of certain productive tasks designed to create a particular condition affecting all parts of the community. Protection from external aggression—the creation of a state of military preparedness—means that the organisation of the whole industrial system must take on a certain character. The end in each of these cases is a complex and integrated whole.

Such ends cannot be brought within the scope and calculus of competition. It is not, of course, impossible to produce in competitive industries any of the separate commodities required by these ends. Antiseptics and armaments, medical and military services could all be produced by competing firms. But the ends themselves—the total states of the economy—cannot be chosen or secured by individual action. They presuppose a social choice. For their achievement the central organisation and control of economic life is essential.

There is no evidence to suggest that these integral or indivisible or social ends are quantitatively less important than divisible or individual ends.

This limitation to the applicability of the theory of competition is much more severe than it looks at first sight. The arrangement of the scarce factors demanded by the social ends may be in conflict with that required by the individual ends. The end of military preparedness, for example, may require the production of wheat to stand in a different quantitive relation to the production of coal from the relation that would be established between them if, as divisible commodities, they are produced under conditions of uncontrolled competition. It is, therefore, impossible to separate off a sphere of economic life peculiarly suited to competitive organisation while leaving a restricted field for the activity of a central authority or state.[1] The existence of satisfaction arising from the total state of the economy may leave no part of it unaffected. Nor is it possible

[1]This implies that the contemporary search for an "agenda for the State" is analytically indefensible.

to dismiss this problem as lying partly within the world of ends. If economics is defined as the study of the arrangement of scarce means with relation to the pursuit of *any* set of ends,[1] it must be relevant to consider the ends which postulate certain relations between all other elements in the economy. The satisfaction obtained from the contemplation of economic justice or the sense of military security is just as much a consumers' satisfaction as the consumption of bread and potatoes. And it arises equally from the distribution of scarce means between alternative uses. Neither production aimed at the satisfaction of such ends, nor the control of the relations between these ends and all others, can possibly be treated by a theory of competitive adjustment. Nor does the existing theory of Public Finance meet the need. The truth is that a theory of competition cannot be made into a theory of general productive equilibrium because it cannot treat certain important types of production at all. For certain types of production the whole economy is the relevant unit.

4 Leaving the existence of integral consumers' ends on one side, it can also be shown that even within the restricted sector of production organised in atomic units, the theory of competitive equilibrium fails to justify the institutions of competition. There is, for example, a striking incompatibility between the conditions that make competition possible and those consistent with the best arrangement of resources. An inescapable dilemma lies hidden in the degree of foresight supposed. If one degree of foresight is assumed, the stability of competitive conditions becomes unlikely. If a less degree is imagined, the correct long-period adjustments cannot be made.

(*a*) If we make the extreme assumption that the individual producer acts *as though his output will have no influence upon the market price*, then it is plainly implied that he must remain ignorant of the true long-period relation between output and price. He is unaware, that is to say, of the reaction of his competitors' supply to the change of price which is common to him and them, and also of the effect on market price of their combined change of output. In these conditions it is impossible for industries to make the correct long-period adjustments. [2]

[1] Professor Robbins' *Nature and Significance of Economics*, passim.
[2] See Mrs. Wootton, *Plan or No Plan*, Chapter II, § 2.

If, for example, there is an increase of demand for a commodity, the price received by the competitive entrepreneurs will rise. They will all assume that the new and higher price will remain unaffected by their individual output policy. Each entrepreneur will raise his output to the point on his marginal cost curve where marginal costs are equal to the new price. He will also begin investments in new fixed capital which are justified, and only justified, on the assumption that the new price is independent of his own output policy. On the same assumption new entrepreneurs will enter the industry. But, of course, the market price is not independent of the output of the industry, and the action of the atomic producers taken together will reduce the market price and falsify the expectations upon which output and investment policy were based. Over-investment will be induced, despite the fact that the increase in demand is itself permanent. As long as the degree of foresight is limited to the assumption of a price dependent on the firm's output policy, the value of the estimated marginal product of resources to the individual entrepreneurs must exceed their true long-period marginal product both to firm and industry.

Two sources of possible confusion should be avoided at this point. The over-investment in fixed capital will not be as great as might at first sight appear. When the demand curve first moves to the right the market price will rise to its highest point. But there will be some immediate increase of output involved in bringing marginal costs up to the new price. Market price will therefore decline from this first high point and investment in new fixed capital will be directed to the short-period equilibrium price and not to the high price that rules the moment after the demand curve has moved to the right. Investment will nevertheless be misdirected. The short-period equilibrium price, which is equal to the marginal cost of output in the existing firms, is still above the price which will rule after the product of the new investment in fixed capital is brought to the market. The final and still lower price will not rule until after the period in which the new investments are completed and the maladjustments irrevocably made.

This is but one example of the confusion and error which must arise if foresight is so limited. For the same reasons, output from competing producers may be increased when demand declines, technical inventions may be over-utilised and cumulative monetary disequilibria generated. The lack of foresight consistent with perfect competition carries with it an appalling blindness of conditioned response.

In the second place, it might be thought that the mere generality of pure competition might prevent the misdirection of investment. This is not the case. A *universal* tendency to over-investment may be checked by the rise in the rate of interest due to the increased demand for new capital. An attempt on the part of all industries to invest more than they should might lead to a correct distribution of the available supply of savings. Indeed if all industries increased their demand for capital in the same degree this would be the case. But it is not *all* industries which are impelled to such investment at each moment of time. On the contrary, only the industries experiencing a present increase of demand will be tempted to over-investment. In a dynamic world, competition of this pure type will induce no tendency to the correct distribution of resources but to a series of over-investment "boomlets" in particular industries. [1]

(*b*) If we turn to the opposite extreme and suppose that individual producers foresee or understand both the true relation between output and market price and the reactions of other producers to price change, it becomes almost impossible to believe that competition itself will be stable. Competition will certainly not continue in so far as the pursuit of private profit is the major incentive of the competitive economy. The moment that all producers become aware of the nature of the demand function and what determines their rivals' output policy, the advantages of monopoly become obvious. Beyond a certain point the extension of foresight and the pursuit of private gain are incompatible with the preservation of competition. It is not necessary to describe at length the maldistribution of resources caused by monopoly.

(*c*) Finally, it may be asked, is there no habitable half-way house between a lack of foresight so complete that wrong invest-

---

[1] For the reality of this process there is much historical evidence. It is, however, difficult to disentangle it from the oscillation of profits attributable to the Trade Cycle. Indeed the tendency for "lack of foresight" booms and slumps in particular industries has often been mistaken for the cause of the Trade Cycle—see Pigou's *Industrial Fluctuations*, Chapters VI and IX, Aftalian's *Les Crises commerciales*, but especially Papi's *Escape from Stagnation*, passim.

ment is inevitable and an understanding so clear that monopoly practices follow upon the pursuit of profit?

It is formally possible that either (*a*) the representative entrepreneur should realise the relation between the market price and the output of the industry but fail to assess the determinants of his rivals' policy, or (*b*) that he should recognise the forces influencing his competitors but not grasp that relation between total output and price. The second of these possibilities is purely formal. If one entrepreneur realises the influence of price upon his rivals' output he must also apprehend the inverse relation between output and price. But the first condition is quite likely to exist, e.g. in many cases of imperfect competition. But it is incompatible with pure competition and, in any case, unlikely to yield any very stable or desirable conditions of production. If there are economies of scale to any firm—and there must be unless every firm has correctly assessed the optimum size of its plant and there has been no variation in the conditions of demand since the plant was built—the circumstances are just those which are likely to result in "cut-throat competition". Producers seeking the economies of scale, or eager to maintain them, will cut prices on the assumption that they will sell more—ignorant of the fact that other producers will follow suit for the same reasons. A cumulative downward movement of prices will begin. Each producer is forced to meet the action of his rivals by similar action and by meeting it frustrates it. Again, it is scarcely necessary to specify the various types of economic loss involved in the existence of imperfect competition.[1]

A stability of competitive conditions *and* a correct distribution of resources under dynamic conditions can only co-exist in the presence of just the degree and type of foresight which will enable entrepreneurs to make correct long-period adjustments and yet fail to appreciate the advantages of monopoly. Such a proposition is purely formal and has no practical meaning whatever. It simply states that if the conditions are such as to lead to the maintenance of equilibrium, equilibrium will be maintained.

[1]See Chamberlain, *Theory of Monopolistic Competition*, Chapter II; Robinson, *Economics of Imperfect Competition*; Kaldor, "Excess Capacity and Imperfect Competition", *Economica*, 1935; etc.

The necessary foresight is that which makes each entrepreneur aware of the price and output reactions of his competitors, but leaves him entirely innocent of the knowledge of monopoly profits and the advantages to be gained by combination. Unless he is imbued with an extraneous enthusiasm for the institutions of *laissez-faire*, such a state of mind is impossible. The theoretical analysis of competitive equilibrium is a two-edged weapon. It can be used to demonstrate the impossibility of equilibrium under competitive conditions. Indeed the definition of the type of foresight required makes it virtually certain that competition and the best arrangement of resources cannot possibly co-exist for long.

5 When we look beyond the formal analysis of competition, the idea of a purely competitive arrangement of resources, and indeed the distinction between a system based upon private enterprise and a socially controlled order, becomes unreal. Not only are the conditions of competition unstable, but even within the field of competitive organisation the force of the social will is present at every point. It is not sufficiently realised that it is quite impossible for the system of consumers' wants and preferances *as a whole* to control the course of production. They are at once too varied and too contradictory. No economy has ever existed or is likely to exist without a selection by custom and law of the ranges of atomic wants which are allowed to impinge upon the market at all. It is not simply that certain ranges of preference are declared illegal or criminal, [1] but that the whole of industrial activity is influenced by laws and customs determining at every point the kind of preference which is to be allowed to exert a direct economic force. It is not economic preferences *as such* which determine the course of competitive enterprise, but only those ranges of preferences which have survived some previous and more fundamental process of social selection. Without a detailed insight into the methods and principles of this selection we can construct no true theory of production and exchange.

Examples of the truth of this assertion exist on every hand. The unpaid costs within our present economy illustrate it. Factory smoke is the standard example. It is possible to build a

---

[1] A fact whose inner economic significance is often neglected by those who construct rationales of *laissez-faire* systems.

factory because cigarettes stand at certain points in the range of preferences of a number of consumers, and because the range of preferences which include the consumption of tobacco is permitted by law and custom to appear in the market. But the same factory is allowed to discharge poisonous fumes into the air and to occupy the only open space in a crowded area without let or hindrance, despite the consideration that the health of hundreds of people will be permanently damaged and that physical health may stand high in the order of consumers' preferences. Why this paradox? Simply because certain ranges of preferences are excluded by law and custom from the cost calculations which determine the distribution of resources. In the same way a speculative builder may plant a house on the skyline of a hill, or in the centre of a stone village, or build a block of offices in the middle of a Regency terrace, because the use of a dwelling or an office stands at a certain position in the scale of preferences of a single individual or corporation. But, in making prior calculations or cost, no allowance is made or need be made for the destruction of natural beauty, the loss of the preferences for harmony felt by thousands of other consumers, nor even for the fall in neighbouring site values. A large proportion of the wanton destruction of our natural and architectural heritage which has characterised the dark age in which we are living is due to the exclusion of these relevant quantities from the scope of market valuation. [1,2]

---

[1] These gross abuses are all examples of Professor Pigou's "divergences between marginal private and marginal social net product" (*Economics of Welfare*, Pt. II). The difference is one of emphasis. Whereas Professor Pigou regards them as chance types of imperfection in calculus, I treat them as examples of the universality of collective choice. Expressed in law or custom these deficiencies of costing are due to the exclusion by society of whole ranges of consumers' preferences from economic calculus. They are not allowed to become effective.

[2] Where a piece of building will reduce the values of other sites, it is, of course, possible for the owners of neighbouring sites to join together to buy up the threatened positions and prevent their uneconomic exploitation. There are, however, a number of reasons for supposing that this possibility will be quite powerless to prevent the misdirection of resources:

(i) The fall in site values, although sufficient, if counted into the cost of building, to render the building economically undesirable, may not be large enough to provide sufficient funds for the purchase of the site. In any case such co-operation is costly to arrange and to finance.

(ii) Many of the affected consumers may have only a negligible interest in the site as individuals although collectively their preferences if organised would be overwhelming. This is typical when a "beauty spot" is destroyed. The loss is suffered by a very large number of people in a very small degree. The organisation of these preferences despite their real significance and overwhelming importance

And there are even wider exclusions than these. Let us take two examples:

1 The abolition of the institution of property in persons has removed from the range of market calculations the relative productivities of investment in human capital. This exclusion has a double result—it creates a bias in favour of investment in physical or non-human factors of production, and it enables entrepreneurs to use up human capital without paying for it. In practice the first of these evils has been corrected in some measure by the growth of public health and educational services. Investment in the improvement of the physical health and intelligence of the working population is financed out of public expenditure because it is excluded from the search for private profit. But its theoretical importance remains. Production and economic calculus are determined at every point by collective decisions.

2 It is a most characteristic feature of our economy that almost no arrangements are made for permitting *negative* preferences to impinge upon the market. It is possible to pay to see a film and thus to cause such a film to be shown and others like to be manufactured. But it is impossible to pay *not* to see a film and so to prevent its manufacture and display. Yet, to judge by the present agitation in America, there are a large number of consumers in whose range of preferences the prevention of certain films stands high. Thus net dissatisfaction may be caused by the display of the film, although its price more than covers its costs of production. If consumers' preferences *as such* were really the arbiter of productive activity, it would obviously be essential to provide a negative box office at every cinema and theatre where people could pay whenever they wished to prevent the performance from taking place! In the same way it is possible to pay for an alcoholic drink and so to keep a beer-house open. It is not possible for a "total abstainer" to pay to have it closed. Indeed if temperance advocates specify too

is impossible upon a competitive basis. *In any case the absurdity lies in the fact that these preferences and the opportunity costs which are associated with them are not automatically charged into the calculations of money cost.* They are just as significant as any other type of loss involved by the use of resources for this given purpose. It is quite absurd to enforce compensation for ancient lights at a distance of ten or twenty feet and not enforce compensation for the loss of æsthetic utilities which may affect the happiness of thousands of people at a mile or two miles from the point of offence.

closely the particular types of beverage or the particular houses of refreshment to which they take objection they are in danger of prosecution for taking part in a "conspiracy in restraint of trade".[1]

These may seem frivolous examples, but there is one substantial member of the group of excluded negative preferences. That is the excluded preferences for *security*. Existing society excludes from its cost calculations the preferences of human beings for stability and certainty. It places a premium upon technical change and economic restlessness. There is no machinery whereby the disutilities suffered by all those who are adversely affected by industrial adaptation can be automatically included in market valuations. Yet they are consumers' preferences and as such relevant to the final decision. This is one of the most dangerous weaknesses of the present order.

It is, therefore, certain that consumers' preferences in their own right are not and cannot be the object of economic activity even in a competitive economy. It is only certain ranges and types of such preferences that are allowed to appear in the field, and the selection of the permitted ranges by law and custom is the underlying determinant of the structure of production. It does not matter, for the thesis of this article, whether the choice is good or bad. Most reasonable men would concede that some of the principles of selection are wise and some are foolish. The essential point is that there *is* a principle of selection. The selection is social in origin. It may be consciously or unconsciously taken, but it is taken by society in its corporate capacity. It is not a response to atomistic individual wants. Any sharp logical distinction between individualist and collectivist economies therefore disappears and we are left with the much more difficult problem of choosing the principles of social selection and resolving the problems of economic calculus in a fundamentally collectivist economy. This is the problem of the real world and the further elaboration of the theory of value upon

[1] I am not, of course, arguing that these negative preferences should be allowed to operate. They would involve an intolerable interference by some persons in other people's freedom of action. In this case the principle of social choice has been wise. It nevertheless remains that production is controlled in this matter—and must continue to be controlled—by a collective decision about ranges of preferences and not by the preferences themselves.

the assumptions of divisible wants and atomistic production can contribute nothing, except indirectly, to its solution. What is urgently required in economic theory to-day is the extension and variation of our institutional postulates in order that economists may formulate and solve the problems of rational calculus in an integrated economy.

ECONOMIC CALCULUS IN A PLANNED ECONOMY

This article (published in 1936) represents my first attempt to apply the theory of pricing and costing to a "planned" or centrally directed economy. It contained a mistake (pointed out by Mr. Lerner in a subsequent number of the "Economic Journal"). I dealt with short period average and marginal costs, in which the size of the operating plant is assumed to be fixed, when I ought to have considered the long period curves in which it is not. My late views on the whole problem are now set forth in the last part of Paper 4 in this book (see footnote on p. 88). I now think that anticipated future average costs are the appropriate guide to pricing policy and investment because all these costs (with negligible exceptions) must, sooner or later, be paid. I have thought it worth including this article, however, because it considers the primary logic of applying the theory of value to a centrally directed economy.

T HE purpose of this article is to demonstrate that there are no theoretical or logical difficulties in the use of an accurate pricing system in a Planned Economy. I accept Mr. Lerner's view that there is no reason to abandon the search for an economic or utilitarian calculus in an industrial system controlled by a central authority. [1] I further concede the argument advanced by Professor Robbins [2] and Professor Hayek [3] that the solution of a system of simultaneous equations by the Central Authority is not a practicable procedure. To this extent I must disagree with the thesis of Mr. Dickinson's original article in this controversy. [4] I am, however, wholly in agreement with him that planned economies differ in no way from *laissez-faire* systems that renders them less suited to solve the

---

[1] Lerner, "Economic Theory and the Socialist Economy", *Review of Economic Studies*, 1935.
[2] Robbins, *The Great Depression*, Chapter VII, § 7.
[3] Hayek, *Collectivist Economic Planning*, V, "The Present State of the Debate", § 3.
[4] Dickinson, "Price in a Socialist Economy", *Economic Journal*, 1933.

problems of economic calculus. The object of this article is to suggest an alternative system to that advanced by him—one that I believe to be more practicable—and so to refute the arguments advanced by Professors Mises, Halm and Hayek in *Collectivist Economic Planning*.[1]

2 The central problem of economic calculus is the familiar second problem derived from the well-established fact of economic scarcity. With the volume of existing resources it is not possible to satisfy all consumers' wants. The first consequent task for society is to diminish this scarcity—the activity of increasing wealth. The second problem is to make the best use in the meantime of the resources we possess—the problem of calculus. Unless democratic doctrine is rejected root and branch, it is necessary to consult the consumers about what they want. There must, therefore, be a free market for consumption goods. If there is to be no wastage of resources, the costs of one commodity must be assessed in quantities of sacrificed alternative goods; there must, therefore, also be a free market for the factors of production. Now, it is the most familiar truism of the theory of value that perfect competition—including perfect foresight—would secure the right adjustment of production to the preferences of consumers. This basic doctrine has been advanced in three separate expositional forms in the history of economic thought, but these three forms are of very different value for resolving the problems of a Planned Economy.

(*a*) The first of them is the traditional Marshallian apparatus of Supply and Demand Curves. In its present form the doctrine asserts that the problem of selection is resolved when, under conditions of perfect competition, marginal revenue is equal to both marginal costs and average costs, including normal profit. Normal profit is so defined as to make the series of propositions arise *ex definitione*—as must be the case in all pure economic theory—but the propositions are none the less illuminating for that.

(*b*) The second form is that used by Professor Cannan in his *Wealth* and by Professor Pigou in the *Economics of Welfare*, and elaborated first in detail by Böhm-Bawerk in the *Positive Theory of Capital*—the solution by way of marginal products. The

---

[1]*Collectivist Economic Planning*, Routledge, *passim*.

problem of selection is said to be resolved when the products at the margin for interchangeable factors in different employments are equal in value. Or, what is the same thing looked at from the point of view of the individual factor, equilibrium is reached when each factor is in the position of maximum net advantage to itself. When every factor is making its greatest possible contribution to the value of the product, the problem of selection is solved.

(*c*) Then there are the equational systems—stating that when competition is perfect, not only is the system of price and quantity equations relating the quantities of the factors, the technical conditions of production and the preferences of the consumers determinate, but also that these prices will resolve the problem of rational choice.

The three forms of the theory of value arrive at the same positive conclusion—that perfect competition secures the right distribution of resources. Do any or all or none of them provide a rule of procedure for the Planned Economy?

3 It is certain that the last method does not! It is true— as Professor Hayek and Professor Robbins argue—that one system of equations could not be completed before another had become relevant. As Professor Hayek says:

"... the magnitude of this essential mathematical operation will depend on the number of unknowns to be determined ... it is hardly an exaggeration to assume that in a fairly advanced society, the order of magnitude would be at least in the hundreds of thousands. This means that, at each successive moment, every one of the decisions would have to be based on the solution of an equal number of simultaneous differential equations, a task which, with any of the means known at present, could not be carried out in a lifetime."[1]

A system of Paretian equations is therefore not available. In the light of the completed argument of this article, however, such a conclusion is more a criticism of the usefulness and realism of the equational method than any blow to the theory of planning.

It is almost equally certain that the second or marginal product method does apply with equal force to either a *laissez-faire* or a planned system. If the Central Authority issues to all production units two instructions: (*a*) that they

---

[1]*Collectivist Economic Planning*, p. 212.

shall calculate the marginal productivity to them of all mobile resources; (*b*) that mobile resources shall everywhere be moved to the positions of highest calculated product; there seems to be no reason to suppose that any different distribution of resources would arise than that arrived at by perfect competition. All logical, theoretical and accountancy problems are common to both types of systems. It may be very difficult to calculate marginal products. But the technical difficulties are the same for capitalist and planned economies alike. All difficulties that are not accountancy difficulties are not susceptible to theoretical dogmatism.

"The calculations will not be made." "The mobile resources will be unwilling to move." "The production units that ought to expand will refuse to do so." All these criticisms may or may not be true. They may or may not be the real problems of policy. But they are not problems that the professor of economic theory is competent to discuss. They are problems of social behaviour. They can only be resolved, if they can be resolved at all, by a comprehensive sociological and principally psychological analysis. As long as the theory of economics consists in the extrapolation or fugual development of a few simple and partially verified assumptions, spurning history and psychology, faltering before the tasks of hypothecation, prophecy and verification, economists may not dogmatise on such practical questions as these. In the realm of economic theory, then, the marginal productivity solution seems adequate. As long as the socialised factories calculate marginal products, and mobile resources continuously move to the highest margins, the problems of calculus will be solved. The ability to discover marginal products is not dependent upon the existence of any particular set of social institutions—certainly not on those of *laissez-faire*.

At the same time the present writer would not be content with any solution concerned exclusively with marginal products, because the movements of resources would have to be based upon *estimated*, and not upon realised marginal products. Now, estimates of marginal value products are extremely liable to error. To discover them the physical result of a radical re-organisation of the production unit must first be estimated. The demand curve for the product must then be calculated.

The margin of error in both calculations is likely to be great, and the resulting value product doubly so.[1] Unless, therefore, the process of continual adjustment and equilibrium of marginal products can be submitted to another type of check and assessment, the problem is only roughly solved. This raises the question of the applicability of the English *cost* analysis to the problems of a Planned Economy.

4 Under conditions of perfect competition, with perfect divisibility of the factors of production and with perfect mobility, all machines will earn "normal profit" upon their cost of production—that is, the Market Rate of Interest upon their cost of replacement. In equilibrium any machine must earn its depreciation allowance and a profit sufficient to prevent the depreciation allowance from being invested elsewhere, and insufficient to cause new capital to come into the industry. The argument used to establish the conclusion is familiar. If the excess of gross receipts over the cost of the non-specific or mobile factors is less than the Market Rate of Interest upon the depreciation allowances continuously re-invested in maintaining the fixed capital, the free money contained in the depreciation allowances could earn a higher reward elsewhere—and will in theory be invested outside the firm and industry, until the industry has shrunk sufficiently to enable the firms remaining in it to earn a normal profit so defined.[2] If the excess of gross receipts over the cost of the mobile resources is greater than Normal Profit, then new capital will flow in, and the industry will be enlarged. In either case with complete mobility the Rate of Interest for the cost of replacement will always be earned. Whether this happens in practice or not it is

[1] For a discussion of this problem in a different context, see my *Problem of Credit Policy*, pp. 81–85.

[2] In practice this will not happen. In the *first* place, the depreciation allowances may never be technically free if the assumption of perfect divisibility is removed. If, for example, the "maintenance of capital" consisted in the replacement of one-tenth of a railway line in each unit period of time, no capital would ever be available for re-investment, because all the capital of the concern would be lost if one or two depreciation quotas were missed. In the *second* place, the allotment of funds between depreciation and profits is normally made by persons—either directors, managers or men who employ themselves—whose chief monetary and psychological interest in the firm arises from their payment and position as employees. Such persons are in the highest degree unlikely to cut the ground from beneath their feet by re-investing the capital elsewhere. In practice, the interest and sentiment of continuity will result in the continuation of the firm as long as it can earn its physical depreciation allowances. Firms will make no net profits indefinitely.

certainly what should happen if the correct distribution of resources is to be made. Does this form of the orthodox theory of value provide any clue for the guidance of a Planned Economy?

Let us now consider the position of a socialised trust. Let us suppose that the Central Authority has instructed all Trusts to compete with each other in the market for the mobile factors of production—land, unspecialised labour and new capital. The market price of the mobile factors will then be equal to their marginal products, and in the particular case of interchangeable factors, equilibrium will be reached when the prices of such factors are everywhere equal. The Central Authority

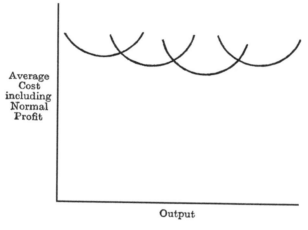

Average Cost including Normal Profit

Output

now wishes to build a factory to produce a new product, or to open a new plant to provide an old product in a new place. In either case it has to construct a plant that will earn a normal rate of profit upon the cost of its construction, i.e. the Rate of Interest established in the free market for new capital existing between the Trusts. But the socialised Trust, since it is in a position of monopoly, is not faced by a horizontal marginal revenue curve. The problem is, therefore, not that of constructing a plant that will maximise profit and leaving the processes of competition to force maximum profit down to a normal or market level, but a more complicated one. With a falling marginal revenue curve it is probable that there are a large number of possible plants of different sizes, all of which would earn normal profits or more. For each possible plant the Trust can estimate:

(*a*) the total overhead cost including a normal profit as defined above;

(*b*) the total cost—and therefore the average cost—of the prime (or mobile) factors required to manufacture a series of outputs on the given plant.

From these two estimates it is possible to draw up the ordinary average overhead and average prime cost curves. When these two are added together, the ordinary **U**-shaped average cost curve for the firm will emerge. There will be a family of such curves varying according to the size of the fixed plant.

The Demand Curve must also be estimated, and for one of the possible sizes of the firms (assuming the possible variations in size to be continuous) the estimated Demand Curve will cut the Average Cost Curve at its minimum point:

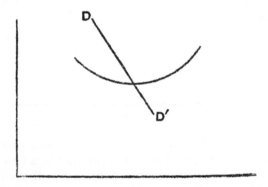

For this point—if the estimates are correct—the price will be equal to average long-period cost including normal profit. This is the correct size for the plant. [1]

[1]It is of importance to remember that the output here described is not the largest output that can earn normal profit. In first thinking of this matter I was led astray by supposing that the ideal to be arrived at by the Socialised Trust was that of producing *the largest physical output upon which normal profit would be earned*. Such a criterion would mean that the Trust would construct a plant for which maximum profit—*i.e.* where the intersection of the marginal cost curve excluding normal profit and the marginal revenue curve—gave a total profit equal to the market Rate of Interest on the cost of constructing the plant. (Cont. on p. 147).

Economic Calculus in a Planned Economy

There is no difficulty about any of these calculations peculiar to the position of a socialised trust. Given the prices of the factors co-operating with the fixed plant—determined in the

The firms owning this plant could—if the estimates were correct—earn normal profit on a relatively large output indefinitely. But it would not—I now think—be the correct output, just because the normal profit is the maximum profit for the plant. *The normal profit can only be obtained on so large a plant because the weapon of monopoly restriction is being used to hold up the net profit to a normal level.* The plant is really too big.

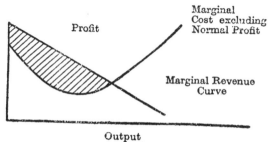

Since maximum profit is the point of intersection between the marginal revenue curve and the marginal prime cost curve, it is necessarily to the left of the minimum point of long-period average cost, including normal profit. The position is this:

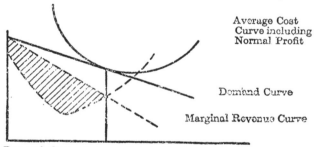

The Demand Curve is tangential to the long-period average cost curve on the left side of its minimum point, and vertically above the point of intersection of the marginal revenue curve and the marginal cost curve, excluding profit. This is not economically desirable, because it involves "excess capacity" in the plant—or a failure to produce at the lowest possible long-period cost including normal profit.

To put the point in another way, investment in this line of production has been carried to such a point that normal profit can only be earned by restricting output. This involves excluding some mobile resources from their most profitable employments in the world of opportunities created by the building of a plant of this size. The alternative was to invest the capital in some other use where it could have earned normal profit without the use of any monopoly power, or the exclusion at any place or time of mobile resources from their highest margins of productivity.

For the clarification of this point—and indeed for the essence of the argument of this section—I am very much indebted to the help of Mr. H. T. N. Gaitskell. His unpublished work in this field is pioneer work, and I could not have written on the subject at all without his aid.

general market for non-specific factors—the estimates are arithmetically possible. Indeed, they are precisely the sort of estimates that would be made by a capitalist firm with a different level of profit (i.e. maximum profit) to aim at. The appropriate plant can therefore be built. If the original calculations were correct, and as long as the data remain unchanged, the margin between gross receipts and total costs will be kept constant, and will be equal to the profit that the competitive firm would have made in the same position, i.e. the market Rate of Interest upon the cost of replacing the capital. But of course the calculations may have been incorrect, and the data will certainly not remain unchanged. We must therefore examine the accountancy position in the socialised unit under dynamic conditions.

The logically separable problems of inaccurate estimates and of subsequent changes in data are, in fact, not analytically different. They both mean that profits are other than normal and that some adjustment is called for. We can therefore consider them together. There are three main types of inaccuracy or change that are worth considering:

(*a*) Demand may have been under- or over-estimated, or it may rise or fall after the plant has been constructed.

(*b*) The prices of the non-specific factors co-operating with the fixed capital may have been wrongly estimated or they may change.

(*c*) The market value of the fixed capital may change either through a change in the market Rate of Interest, or through invention, or through technical obsolescence.

What are the adjustments that should be made if any of these changes occur? Let us consider them one at a time:

(*a*) Suppose that demand increases. The demand curve will rise, and if the costs of the non-specific factors and the cost of physical depreciation remain constant, the amount of net profits will rise. They will rise to a new and higher maximum if output is expanded until marginal cost is equal to the new marginal revenue. They will rise to a higher level on the old minimum cost output, and to a new potential maximum if output is expanded to the new point of intersection between the marginal revenue curve and the marginal cost curve. Since the cost of replacement is constant and the market Rate of Interest assumed to be unchanged, normal profit is unaltered, while realisable money profits are up. The realisable rate of profit on a range of outputs is in excess of the normal rate of profit. Equilibrium plainly requires an increase of fixed capital. Whether the increase of output should be secured by enlarging the existing plant or by building a new one, is simply a problem of securing the minimum total cost including normal profit. Whatever the output that will earn normal profits in the new expanded market may be, it should be produced at *lowest total cost*. Whether the lowest cost will be reached in one production plant or two is a purely technical problem to be resolved by an inquiry into total costs. No difficulty therefore arises from applying a cost analysis to the circumstances of an expanding market.

(*b*) The case when *demand decreases* is more difficult because two alternative policies are open to the Trust. The marginal revenue curve is now lower, and profits are below normal. Under competition one of two courses would be pursued. Either the owners of the fixed plant would at once begin to withdraw their capital and re-invest it elsewhere. In this case profits will be restored to normal for the surviving capital. Or they may continue to maintain their capital physically intact, and content themselves with carrying production to the point of maximum net profit in the new position—the point where marginal revenue is equal to marginal cost excluding profit. The owners can continue to pursue the second course indefinitely, as long as the fall in demand is not sufficiently severe to cut into the allowances for physical depreciation. Production and re-investment in the plant would then continue indefinitely at less than normal profit. [1]

What is the position of the socialised plant faced by a similar decline in demand? It need not seek to maximise its profits, so that the choice before it is somewhat different. The plant can no longer earn its normal profit, but the management could proceed as under the second case of competition—and carry production to the point of maximum profit where marginal revenue was equal to marginal costs. In this case, as under competition, they could remain indefinitely earning less than normal profit. Such a position would not be one of long-period

[1] The second course would, in my view, be the normal procedure for a firm operated by the legal method of Joint Stock enterprise. See footnote on p. 144.

equilibrium, because the resources attached to the production unit would be idle. The production unit would not be working at the capacity that originally returned the normal profit upon its cost of replacement. In the long period it would be necessary to adapt the plant to the lower output made necessary by the fall in demand.

But this is not the only possible course open to the responsible Authority. Since it is not under the necessity of maximising profit, it could instruct the firm to carry production to the point at which *price* covered marginal cost. As long as the plant is regarded as a technical fixture equivalent to land (bygones being bygones) this is the theoretically desirable course. Price covers the cost of the mobile factors, and these are brought at once to their highest margins. In all cases the execution of this policy would mean carrying production beyond the point where marginal revenue was equal to marginal cost. Maximum profits would never be made. Indeed, the general direction given to the production units might quite often involve them in incurring large losses.[1] Since, however losses in one direction would always be offset by equal profits elsewhere as long as total expenditure were constant, the policy would not be impracticable for a Central Authority owning all industries, although it might be impracticable if anything less than everything were in the hands of the State.[2]

Now, for two important reasons of different kinds, I believe that the first general directive on accounting and production policy is, in practice, the better to issue:

> (*a*) The order to carry production to the point where price is equal to marginal prime cost can be justified only upon the assumption that it is possible to distinguish between the payment of prime costs and the maintenance of fixed capital. Unless this is possible, production will continue indefinitely at the old level. The decision to change the scale of output will be made when the existing machines come to be

[1] On a railway, for example, the marginal prime cost of carrying passengers or goods is often—indeed, usually—nothing. In such cases as this criterion prices should be zero and the line should make a loss equal to its total costs. Of course the marginal cost of running an extra train is not zero. In practice the results of the policy would entirely depend on the definition of the *unit of output*. If the unit of output was a "passenger mile", marginal cost would be zero; if it were a "train mile", it would be appreciable; while if it were a mile of railway, it would be greater still. The general directive in this case would lack all precision.

[2] I am indebted to Mr. Lerner for a discussion of this particular point. He is not, however, responsible for my views, as I believe that he disagrees with the conclusions that I have come to on this particular point.

replaced and cease to be bygones. But, in fact, no such clear distinction exists. A railway, for example, maintains its permanent way continuously. It would not be possible to distinguish between the current payments that were true prime costs and those that involved the maintenance of capital. Thus the instruction not to restrict output and to continue the payment of current costs because the capital was there would often involve the maintenance of redundant capital indefinitely. The maximisation of profit will possess the advantage of revealing automatically the existence of surplus capacity.

(*b*) In the second place, the first set of instructions issued has the great practical advantage of simplicity. The Central Authority simply says to its local representatives: "Here is a plant. Whatever output you make, make it at the lowest possible total cost. Make the largest output you can consistent with earning normal profit on the cost of replacing your plant. When, through a change in market conditions, you cannot earn normal profit at all, then earn the biggest profit you can (i.e. produce at the point where marginal revenue is equal to marginal cost other than profit). When you cannot earn normal profit, you will be producing less than the capacity for which the plant was built, and you must then consider what smaller plant would, working to capacity, produce a lower output and earn normal profit. In the fullness of time that plant must be built." Such a general instruction would have the great advantage that it would enable the management to meet changes in market conditions independently, and without the complex system of taxes and bounties required by the other instruction. It would, however, mean a continuous wastage of fixed plant in the industries suffering from a decline in demand. The size of this margin of waste would vary with the extent of the change in demand and the length of the average period before fixed capital were replaced.

Apart from difficulties of accountancy, common to planned and unplanned economies alike, and apart from the resistance to change of any kind—a question of social behaviour not susceptible to the categories of economic theory—there is, then, no insuperable problem in adjusting a Planned Economy to changes in demand.

(*c*) Other types of change can be treated more summarily. They all involve a change in the relationship within the production unit between the level of realised profits and the level of normal profits. The *prices of the non-specific and mobile resources may rise or fall.* If the price of labour rises, for example, the level of realised profits will fall. If this is a general movement —if wages are rising everywhere—then the external rate of normal profits will fall. In the production units employing a large amount of labour, realised profits will fall below the new and lower level of normal profits, and a position will arise similar to that arising from a decline in demand. Production must be contracted, and in the long run a new plant earning normal profit must be built. If the rise in the prices of mobile factors is not general, but restricted to the particular kind of labour employed in the affected industry, the level of realised profits will fall relatively to that of normal profits unequivocally and at once, and the same problem of adjustment will arise. If the prices of the primary factors decline, then profits will rise, and the simpler problems of expansion can be solved.

Finally, *technical conditions may change*—giving rise to technical obsolescence in the plant. Obsolescence may take one of two forms—either the new forms of capital cost less than the old, or they will require an investment of new capital. In the first case, the old depreciation allowances will buy new machines and still leave a net profit above the surrounding rate of normal profit. The same fundamental problem of expansion that we have already discussed then appears. In the second case, as long as the reduction in costs through the installation of the new capital gives a margin of profit equal or superior to the level of normal profits, the installation should, of course, proceed.

There are, then, no dynamic changes that are not immediately reflected in the relation between prices and costs, and which do not subsequently reveal the nature of the desirable adjustments by a change in the relationship between the level of realised profits and the level of normal profits. By observing the changing relationship between surplus receipts within and without the unit of production, simple economic calculus would then seem possible in a Planned Economy.

5 This conclusion is radically opposed to the argument advanced by Dr. Hayek in his recent publications on the subject.[1] He rejects the view that marginal costs can be used to guide the distribution of resources in a Planned Economy, because he denies that "money costs" possess any clear and definite meaning—or can be precisely evaluated. This is what he says in the critical passage of his article:

[1] *Collectivist Economic Planning, The Present State of the Debate,* and particularly § 8, on "The Criterion of Marginal Costs".

Economic Calculus in a Planned Economy

"It is in this connection that it almost seems as if perhaps some excessive pre-occupation with the conditions of a hypothetical state of stationary equilibrium has led modern economists in general, and especially those who propose this particular solution, to attribute to the notion of costs in general a much greater precision and definiteness than can be attributed to any cost phenomenon in real life. . . . Much of what is usually termed cost of production is not really a cost element that is given independently of the price of the product, but a quasi-rent, or a depreciation quota which has to be allowed on the capitalised volume of expected quasi-rents, and is therefore dependent on the prices which are expected to prevail. . . . These quasi-rents . . . are not a less reliable and indispensable guide for the determination of the appropriate volume of production than true cost. On the contrary, it is only in this way that some of the alternative ends which are affected by the decision can be taken into account. Take the case of some unique instrument of production which will never be replaced and which cannot be used outside the monopolised industry, and which therefore has no market price. Its use does not involve any costs which can be determined independently from the price of its product. Yet if it is at all durable and may be used up either more or less rapidly, its wear and tear must be counted as true cost if the appropriate volume of production at any one moment is to be rationally determined . . ."[1]

Part of Dr. Hayek's complaint—the excessive preoccupation with static conditions—has already been met in this article. We have considered all the significant types of change to which the production unit can be submitted. But Professor Hayek goes on to claim that the analysis is built upon sand because important groups of money costs are not determined independently of prices. There are factors whose prices cannot be derived from any source outside the market for their own special product.

Is there any substance in this charge? Is there any important group of factors that cannot be valued by any independent process whatever? Let us review the factors of production from this point of view. No problem arises from the group of mobile or non-specific factors of production. For them, transfer prices are equal to their marginal productivities, and these are determined in the general market for mobile resources that we have assumed to exist between the Socialised Trusts. Their prices are therefore independent of the prices of the particular product of their present employment. Neither is there

[1] *Op. cit.*, pp. 226–228.

any difficulty over depreciating factors. However specific a factor might be in the short period—a machine capable of one process, for example—as long as it wear out, the depreciation allowance made for it continuously converts it into a non-specific factor. As a non-specific factor the free capital continuously invested in the maintenance of the specific machine —or skilled labour—must receive its transfer price, i.e. the normal market rate of profit on free capital. The only type of factor that could possibly give rise to any difficulty is a factor that is both specific and non-depreciating or eternal.

Now, are there really many such factors? There are many specific factors—most machines and skilled labour are highly specific—but they all rapidly depreciate or die. There are many eternal factors—all sites, for example—but they are rarely specific. One of the fundamental technical reasons for the frequency with which rents are legally compulsory payments is the great mobility of sites between different employments. The land market is likely to be particularly real in the economic as well as the legal sense.

Is not the category of specific and eternal factors really an empty one? A group of persons trying to think of an actual factor of production that was both highly specific and non-depreciating could only think of a railway tunnel through very hard rock! But even this example is of no use to Professor Hayek. For, after all, what is the importance of pricing such factors? Since they are specific, they can only be used in one employment. Since they are eternal, they cost nothing to maintain. The only importance of pricing them is to prevent the over-utilisation of the more efficient among them. If no rent is charged, production will be carried to the point at which the average cost of the non-specific factors on the superior examples of the specific factor is equal to the cost of the non-specific factor on the inferior examples—an undesirable distribution of the non-specific factors.[1] Hence maladjustment will only take place when there is a group of the same specific factors all eternal, but differing amongst themselves in productivity. What Professor Hayek requires to prove his argument is not one tunnel through hard rock leading from one place to another,

[1] See the discussion of the problem of utilising superior and inferior free roads by Professor Pigou and Professor Knight.

but a bunch of tunnels all conveying traffic between the same two places—and all through very hard rock! Until it has been shown that such peculiar groups of factors are quantitatively significant no important gap in the pricing system here proposed has been discovered.

6 I have only attempted in this article to demonstrate the theoretical possibility of a pricing system in a Planned Economy —a possibility that has been dogmatically denied by Professor Mises and others. [1] There is, I contend, no ground for such a view. The real arguments for and against planning lie elsewhere. The main charge offered by economists against a Planned Economy—that it has no method at its disposal for the rational calculation of relative productions—is, however, refuted.

This result is of considerable importance for those who believe that a Planned Economy can—through the greater power to vary the money income of the community possessed by a unified investing and saving authority, through the better and juster type of society that could be raised upon its foundations, and in general through the superiority of conscious reason over blind instinct in the achievement of any end whatever— be made into a better economy than a *laissez-faire* economy can ever hope to be. But these are wider and more practical questions. Social science, and not economic theory, can alone hope to find an answer to them.

[1] See particularly *Collectivist Economic Planning*, pp. 104–5, for an amazing example of uncritical dogmatism on this point.

ECONOMICS

Paper IX

THE NATURE OF ECONOMICS

The last group of three papers deals with some of the problems of economics as a science. The first of them deals in a simple way with the nature of the scientific method and the problems of applying that method to the study of social problems—and an assessment of the extent to which economics and the other social sciences have made use of it in the past.

Introduction

THE public estimation of economics and economists contains a curious paradox. In one sense economics has come into its own during the last few years. Economists are appointed to every conceivable advisory and administrative board and committee from government departments downwards. Papers and periodicals are full of articles on economic and financial subjects. Economic explanations of this and that, of war and crime and political change, are at a premium. The university courses in the subject are crowded with an embarrassingly large flood of students. Economics is the intellectual religion of the day.

At the same time there is a widespread irritation with the present state of the subject and a growing criticism of its methods of work. It is contrasted most unfavourably with the physical sciences and many people are coming to the view that it is not a science at all.

The contrast is certainly startling. The natural scientist—the physicist or the chemist or the botanist—can achieve results that are quite beyond the economist or the student of politics or the social psychologist.

The astronomer can predict, with absolute accuracy and (so far) with complete certainty, that an eclipse of the sun will begin at 11.31 a.m. precisely on October 31st, 2047. The physicist can make an instrument that, without sight or sound, can foretell the approach of an aeroplane a hundred miles away. The chemist can say that wherever and whenever a solution of (shall we say) calcium sulphate is added to a solution of sodium chloride an amount of calcium chloride will be deposited at the bottom of the containing vessel. In fact, scientific students of the physical world can make most accurate prophecies about the future course of events, prophecies that are always true and have been verified a thousand times. As a result, they are able to give us an ever-growing command over the natural world—aeroplanes and rockets, the cure of disease, a great increase in industrial productivity and a vast extension of human power over material things.

How different is the position of the social sciences! In 1930 the late Lord Keynes, the most famous economist then living, prophesied that the fall in prices on the New York Stock Exchange would soon stop and would be followed by a rapid recovery and a large industrial expansion. But stock prices continued to fall steeply for the next two years, and the world was plunged into the worst depression in living memory. Keynes was exactly wrong. In the same way almost no student of politics (including myself) had the slightest idea that the outcome of the 1945 General Election in Britain would be a landslide to Labour. Indeed, the most careful investigator of these matters that I know, who had been very accurate in his forecasts of previous general elections, foretold a Conservative majority of more than one hundred and fifty! The contrast between the accuracy and universality of the findings of the physical sciences on the one hand, and the uncertainty, inaccuracy and unreliability of the statements made by social scientists could scarcely be more complete.

It is not surprising, therefore, that those who are familiar with the remarkable achievements of the natural sciences should complain about the unsatisfactory state of economics and should go on to accuse the social scientists of making a muddle of their job and failing to use truly scientific methods in their work.

This leads us at once to consider the two questions with which this chapter is chiefly concerned. Is economics a science? And, if so, why do its results lack the prophetic accuracy and the universality of the discoveries made in physics, chemistry, botany or astronomy?

The Nature of Economics

Is Economics a Science

My own answer to this question is yes—but before it is possible to explain why I think so, it is necessary for us to be clear what we mean by a science.

A science, it will be generally agreed, is the result of applying a certain fundamental method of thought to some definite field of human experience. Physics is the result of applying that method to a study of physical objects, botany is the result of applying the same method to the study of plants, astronomy to the study of the stars—and so through the list of all the sciences. It is a *method of study* that is common to all these different subjects, and it is the nature of this method we must understand.

What then, is the scientific method? It is easiest to answer this question by considering two practical examples of it in action. Let us, for example, examine Newton's formulation of the law of gravity and Fleming's discovery of penicillin, as cases in point:

What was it that Newton did to advance the basic study of physics when he conceived the theory of gravitational attraction? First he surveyed the great number of observations that had been made of the appearances of the heavenly bodies. He did not make all these observations himself—although he made some. For hundreds of years men had been seeing, noting and recording the movements of the sun, the moon and the stars. This led to the accumulation of a great number of facts ("empirical observations" to use the jargon of the scientists) that needed to be explained. Using his imagination and his powers of reason, Newton said to himself: "All these movements of these lights in the sky and the falling of objects towards the centre of the earth would be 'explained' if it were true that bodies in space attract each other in proportion to their weight and in inverse proportion to the square of the distance between them." This was his famous theory, the "principle of gravity". But he did not stop there. He went on to say: "If my theory is true, and if physical bodies so attract one another, then it will necessarily follow that the pace at which objects fall to the earth will be accelerated at a certain rate, and the curious movements of the planet Saturn can best be explained by the existence of another unseen planet revolving round the sun at a greater distance from it than Saturn." Subsequent work by physicists and astronomers showed that both these logical deductions from the theory of gravity were, in fact, accurate. Objects did fall with the velocity deduced by Newton; the planet Neptune was, in fact, discovered later, just where he estimated it to be. In short, Newton's theory was verified by further observations.

But it is necessary, also, to notice the ultimate fate of his theory. In one sense, it lasted, almost unchallenged, for three hundred years. During that time, however, there slowly accumulated a number of observations or facts (the movements of Saturn's moons for example) that did not square with the Newtonian formula for gravity; and so Einstein, some thirty years ago, worked out another piece of mathematics—called the theory of relativity—that brought these exceptions into a more general mathematical formula, of which Newton's theory of gravity is a particular example. Einstein's theory has, in turn, been verified by further astronomical observations and no doubt will be replaced in turn by still more general theories in the future.

A somewhat simpler case is to be found in the discovery of penicillin. It had long been observed that dead bodies, filled with every kind of infection (pneumococcus, streptoccus and staphylococcus) did not corrupt the soil of graveyards. In 1928 Sir Alexander Fleming noticed in his laboratory that a culture plate of staphylococcus had become contaminated with a mould which, when it had grown, put a stop to all bacterial development in its immediate neighbourhood. Using the power of his imagination and reasoning Fleming argued: this would happen if it were the case that this mould (*Penicillium notatum*) produced substances that kill, dissolve or inhibit the multiplication of the bacterial cells. He and Sir H. W. Florey went on to verify this theory by extracting penicillin and with it counteracting the effects of bacterial infection, first in test tubes, then in the blood of animals and finally in the living bodies of human beings, with the splendid medical results of which we are now aware—results which mark the greatest advance in phenomenology for fifty years.

We are not, of course, concerned here with these scientific discoveries themselves, but with the method of thought that is common to them both. It consists, as the reader will see, of three essential and inseparable steps.

First comes observation. Newton sees objects falling to the earth; he takes note of the innumerable astronomical observations made by other men since the dawn of history. Fleming sees through his microscope that the staphylococci are dead and that the strands of penicillin are present. This is where it must all begin. The facts must be experienced and recorded. Sometimes the observations are simple and made by the unaided senses. Anyone of normal sight can see the movements of the stars and the nearer planets. Anyone can notice that the soil of graveyards is not infectious. In other cases the necessary observations can only be made by elaborate and sensitive instruments—telescopes and microscopes that magnify points of light many hundred times; seismographs that detect tremors of the earth at a distance of five thousand miles; scales that can weigh to the thousandth of an ounce; instruments that record electrical impulses to the millionth of a volt. But in all cases the process is the same—the impartial observation and accurate recording of the impressions made upon the physical senses. Science begins with the facts.

But the observed facts would be meaningless without the other powers of the human mind. The second step is to use the faculty of imagination and the gift of reason to offer some explanation of why the observations are what they are, and why they are related to one another as they are. Newton must sit down (as he did for five months at Cambridge) and say, "If all the bodies in space attracted one another directly in proportion to their mass and inversely to the square of the distance between them it would follow that. . . ." He must sweep the universe with his mind to conceive a general explanation (a hypothesis, as it is called) and then use his reason to show, by logical steps, that all the observations would follow consistently from the point of this theory.

Fleming must not only see that the staphylococci are dead but also imagine that this is so because penicillium secretes invisible substances that kill them. Imagination and pure reason come into their own (little as some natural scientists realise it) at this stage of the scientific process.

Finally, it is necessary to proceed to the verification of the theory. The work of science is not complete until new evidence can be produced to show that the theory works, that is, until it is shown that the theory can be used to make observations that have never been made before. Newton, or his successors, must show that bodies actually move towards the centre of the earth at the pace logically consistent with the theory of gravity. Astronomers of future generations must turn their telescopes to points in space-time and see the planet Neptune that had never been seen before. Fleming and Florey, and their collaborators, must inject penicillin into rats and see the fevers of pneumonia die away. This is the final duty and reward of the scientist in action—a theory justified.

And it is the fate of the true scientist—at once sad and challenging—that his work is never done, his results never final. A theory may stand for three hundred years. But one day it will be replaced. It was always wrong, too limited, eternally provisional. The mystery of the universe still remains. The questing mind moves on—farther and deeper—to a receding goal. Science, in a word, is progressive.

Is this also true of the social sciences in general and of economics in particular?

It should be obvious that, little as many economists understand it, this threefold method of observation, reasoning and verification is the only solid method available to them for the study of their own field of inquiry.

Let us consider the application of this fundamental method to two of the problems central to economics and dealt with in various chapters of this book—the trade cycle that characterizes the capitalist system and the problem of industrial incentives.

It has long been known that the capitalist system, while continuously expanding, suffers from a mysterious rhythm of industrial activity. At one moment prices, profits, income and employment are high and increasing. At another they are rapidly declining. These phases last for some time, succeed one another, and in passing from boom to depression make much of the history of modern society, including often the immediate causes of some devastating war—for example, the rise of Hitler to power in Germany.

The gradual appreciation of this fact has been one of the main discoveries of modern economics and large amounts of money and time have been given, particularly in the United States, to investigating and recording the movements of the forces at work—prices, rates of interest, volumes of production and expenditure, bank clearings, money income and the rest of it. This is the first stage of the scientific method—observation.

Someone must then sit back to survey the growing body of facts—and many economists did—and conceive an explanation of them—a theory that would logically account for them all. In the case we are considering, that of the trade cycle, the most commonly accepted explanation was that of the alternating excess and deficiency of investment in relation to saving by the consuming public, and the amount spent by industrialists with the Government on new investment. I am not concerned with the truth or detail of this theory but with the nature of the mental processes used in its construction—and this is clearly the second stage of the method—employing imagination and reason for the construction of a hypothesis.

And then it is necessary to attempt some kind of verification. It is possible for the economist to say: "If I am right, and the trade cycle is due to variations in investment, then it will be possible for me to take the statistics of a particular country, not one of those already examined, but known to be subject to the cycle, and to show that, in fact, the volume of investment changes in the cyclical fashion required by the theory." Such a test and such a proof would correspond to astronomical prophecy of the existence of Neptune, whereby the theory of gravity was verified. Or the economist could proceed along the practical road. He could say—if my theory is true, then it must follow that if steps are taken to maintain investment at a sufficiently high level, the disastrous down-swings of the trade cycle will be prevented and general unemployment will disappear. Such a process of reasoning, if accurate, would correspond with the medical proof, through the cure of pneumonia, that the substances produced by penicillin were fatal to the life of the coccal bacteria.

And it is certain that this threefold process of economic enquiry is progressive and never-ending; that the final truth is never known; that behind each mystery there lies a greater one; and yet that progress is made and knowledge grows.

In the same way it is of the greatest theoretical and practical importance to resolve the problems of incentive in economic life—to discover what will induce people to work hard and will reconcile them to the discipline of group activity within the factory. Again the scientific method is available and is, alone, likely to yield results. The conditions of employment must be observed—the way in which reward is linked to the effort, the existing forms of leadership and discipline, the conditions of light and humidity. All these factors must be described, measured, recorded and related to performance and output. From these observations a number of theories will result; for example, that men and women work better under a system of piece rates; that they work better when they are consulted and praised; that they work better if they are kept warm and comfortable. These are hypotheses that can be, and are, tested in practice by the enlightened managements of factories and offices, and proved either true or false.

Thus it will be seen that in the large-scale problems of the whole system, and in the more limited questions that arise within small parts of it, the three-phase scientific method is available to economists and, in so far as they make use of it, establishes their subject as a science and confers upon their findings the passing authority of growing knowledge.

This is the answer to the question with which we started.

Two further points about the method of economics must, however, be made before we pass on to other subjects.

First, it is interesting to notice that many economists do not understand the nature of the argument that has just been advanced, and that the futility of much past and present economics can be traced to this failure on their part.

Very few economists have grasped the necessity for combining observation with reason and verification. They have tried to separate them and, worse still, to praise one activity at the expense of the other. Many economic historians and statisticians have tended to worship the accumulation of "facts" and to decry "theory". As a consequence they have assembled vast piles of meaningless figures and observations for which they offer no explanation whatever. In half a dozen books by American statisticians, for example, representing the expenditure of untold energy and of research grants running into tens of thousands of dollars, in which there are thousands of elaborate statistical calculations, not a single chapter or paragraph attempts to explain *why* these figures are what they are. This is blind and purposeless work, leading nowhere. Observation without reason is a meaningless burden upon the memory.

In Britain, economics has suffered from exactly the opposite mistake. Economists have concentrated upon pure reason to the exclusion of fact and test. The science has been cursed with an excess of theory. For a hundred years most English economists have been content to reason upon the basis of classical economics, weaving elaborate problems of logic upon a few assumptions that had never been properly established and were no longer true (I speak as a sinner in this myself).

When Ricardo and John Stuart Mill wrote their books over a hundred years ago it was not unreasonable to assume that industry was privately owned and competitive; that wage rates fell everywhere, until there was full employment; that the main purpose of banking and monetary policy was to maintain the gold standard. But it is a strange and pathetic obsession to base ever more complicated and subtle formulae upon these assumptions decades after industry has passed into the hands of joint stock companies and public monopolies, is dominated by fixed costs and large-scale unemployment, and has long ceased to make use of any form of gold standard. It is not that the ordinary textbooks of economics are wrong—the logic is often elaborately correct—but that they are so largely irrelevant to the world in which we live, and give the subject of economics a remote and unconvincing sound wholly missing from other sciences firmly based upon fresh observations and accumulating facts.

Of course, this is not true of all economics or economists. The study of the trade cycle, to which I have referred, and most of the work on money and on foreign trade, has always been scientific in the full sense of the term. Here "theory" has never been divided from history and statistics, and has never been lacking in immediate practical application. But in much of the rest of the field, particularly in that part of it (called the principles of economics) which is concerned with the use of economic resources, the divorce is very nearly complete. Consider two examples.

The account of the way in which the capitalist system works

depends on the assumption that the "employer" is kept efficient and adaptable by the search for profit. But this theory wholly ignores the fact that joint-stock enterprise has come to dominate the field and that, in the case of medium- or large-scale firms, all the work of management is carried out by salaried employees who are in no way affected by the level of profits. The profits, in fact, are paid to the shareholders, who contribute nothing to the administration of the concern. Profits have ceased to be a personal motive for ninety-nine out of every hundred persons responsible for the policy of large-scale industry. The old assumption has long since ceased to be true, and the elaborate theorizing based upon it has become wholly unscientific. In the same way it had been assumed from the beginning of economics that those who invest money do so because they see a difference between the increase in the profits they expect to make and the interest that will have to be paid on borrowed money. Yet an incomplete study carried out in the University of Oxford showed that not one in sixteen of the firms consulted paid any attention whatever to the rate of interest! In both these cases it is a failure to combine observation with reason, or test out a theory in practice, that explains the failure of these branches of economics to rise to the level of a science or carry conviction in the public mind.

Marxist economists are in a different case. There is nothing wrong with their theory or method. They begin with the facts. Marx and Lenin were both economic historians. They are prepared, indeed determined, to use reason to explain the facts of history. They offer a whole set of theories to account for everything, from unemployment to prostitution. They even accept, most rare of all, the obligation to verify their theories or, at least, to offer some evidence that they are true. The Marxist and communist doctrine of "the unity of theory and practice" is, after all, nothing more than a political way of stating the truth about scientific method: if a theory is true, then it must work in practice and fulfil itself in action. And if one is not prepared to act upon a theory, it must be because one does not really believe it to be true.

Despite all these positive virtues the Marxist economists—at least the modern ones—are not scientific and in many ways are the least scientific of all. And that is because they do not accept the final test of science, its own self-destructive progressiveness. No one can be a scientist who does not begin by admitting that all his theories are necessarily wrong, in the sense that they will be modified out of all recognition by the development of his own studies. No scientist can be dogmatic, yet every Marxist is —with disastrous consequences. For example, the very basis of his theory has been undermined by the work of modern psychology. The Marxist analysis depends upon the theory that human beings are chiefly controlled by economic or "materialist" motives. They believe in the "materialist interpretation of history". Yet Freud and the psycho-analysts have shown, almost beyond dispute, that the behaviour of men and women is most deeply affected by quite different emotional forces: feelings that are anything but economic, that are scarcely rational and mostly below the level of consciousness. All this the Marxist must either deny or ignore in order to maintain the purity of his Marx-worship and the integrity of his closed circle of reasoning on assumptions passing as swiftly out of date as those of his old enemy, the classical economist.

Nevertheless, despite the ignorance and prejudice of many economists and schools of economic thought, the main scientific value of economics remains; and this at once raises my second point. If it is the case that economics can, and in certain fields does, apply the three-phase method of science, why it is that the results of its studies lack the certainty and universality of the natural sciences? Why is it that astronomers can foretell the future with complete accuracy, and economists cannot? Why do the laws of chemistry apply always and everywhere, while the laws of economics change continually? This is the next main question to which we must turn.

Economics and Human Nature

The biological sciences are concerned with living bodies and forces and as a result, are in many ways intermediate between the physical sciences and the social sciences.

The social sciences in general, and economics in particular, differ from the natural sciences in the nature of the objects they study. The physical sciences are concerned with material bodies and forces: with sticks and stones, liquids and gases, stars and electricity. The social sciences are concerned with human beings. This makes all the difference between the kinds of results that can be obtained from the two sets of subjects.

Human beings differ in a number of obvious and vital ways from material bodies and forces, though this is often forgotten by industrialists. They think and feel and act in a way that stones and gases and electricity do not. But they differ from material objects in one certain, and in one highly probable, way that makes an inescapable and all-pervading difference to the results of studying their behaviour.

First, *human beings can learn from their own experience*. And this makes all the difference to the predictability of their actions.

The story begins with quite humble animals. Dogs and horses can change their behaviour according to their past experience of the world in which they live. They can learn to avoid foods that poison them. They can acquire the habits of responding to bells or sights or words of command that they associate with rewards or punishments. They possess, in short, the elementary processes of memory, reason and intelligence. These powers are much more highly developed in other animals, particularly rats and monkeys. The observation of animal behaviour shows quite considerable capacities for reason and learning in the animal kingdom.

Among men these gifts undergo a revolutionary extension and improvement. The immense increase in the size of the brain and the higher nerve centres brings with it a vast capacity (in comparison with animals) for remembering, reasoning, judging and choosing. These are the essential characteristics of all humanity, little as the present state of the world may seem to justify such a view.

But this fact makes a profound difference to the result of applying the scientific method to a study of creatures such as ourselves. The basic assumption of the natural sciences—that the same causes or conditions will always lead to the same results or outcome—at once disappears, and the possibility of discovering universal laws goes for ever.

Let me illustrate what I mean.

The law of gravity states that all physical bodies at *all times and in all places* will attract one another with a force proportionate to their mass and in inverse proportion to the square of the distance between them. It is possible for the physicist to say that water (of a certain degree of purity and at a certain pressure) will turn to steam if raised to boiling point *anywhere and at any time*. It is not open to stars to dislike one another and to repel each other, instead of mutually attracting one another. A kettle of water cannot decide that it does not like being boiled and get up and walk away. Consequently it is the basic assumption of astronomy and physics, verified a thousand times, that the same causes will produce the same results—that the outcome of a situation is independent of the past "experience" of the physical bodies affected by it.

Exactly the opposite is true of human beings. A boy who gets his fingers burned at a fire will not touch the fire again. He has learned by experience that the result of doing so are unpleasant. All the surrounding conditions may be the same. The fire may be in the same grate; it may be of the same size, shape and brightness; the boy may be just as cold. Yet the result will be exactly the opposite. Instead of touching the live coals the boy will draw back his hand. Indeed, the more similar the conditions, the less the effort of memory and the more likely it is that the result will be different. Hence it becomes quite impossible to say: "All little boys, of a certain age, placed at a certain distance from a fire of a given intensity will touch it." Far from it. All that can be said is that under these conditions some boys will burn their fingers and some will not, according, in part at least, to the nature of their previous experience of fire. The outcome of any set of conditions in which human beings are the subject of study will depend as much upon the past history and experience of the human beings in question as upon anything else.

All this applies directly to the larger problems of human behaviour studied by the economist and social scientist.

Let us revert to the trade cycle. Suppose for a moment that the saving-investment theory of these cyclical movements of prosperity and employment has been true in the past, and that unemployment rises with a fall of investment. If economics were like physics, and human beings resembled bricks or pebbles, then it would be possible to say: "Wherever and whenever investment falls below the intended level of saving then unemployment or cumulative depression will follow." The same causes will always lead to the same results.

But in the life of human society, and of nations, it is plainly not possible to say anything of the kind. Depressions have occurred before. Particular nations have suffered the dreary consequences of prolonged mass unemployment. The child has burned his fingers at the fire. As a result men and women have been commissioned to study these events, to reflect upon their causes and to recommend a cure. Theories of depression have been worked out, policies have been evolved and, perhaps, the necessary arrangements made to carry them out. In this particular case, for example, steps may be taken to increase public investment or private consumption to offset a fall in private investment. If all this has happened the same effects will *not* follow the same causes. The first decline in capital expenditure will not be followed by spreading and deepening depression and rising unemployment, but by a rise in other forms of spending, a maintenance of total expenditure and full employment. The old sequence between cause and effect has been broken by the human power to learn from experience.

In the same way and for the same reason it is never possible to be dogmatic about the future history of any nation. It is out of the question, for example, to say (as the Marxists say) that *all* nations will abandon political democracy if they attempt to replace a capitalist system by a socialist economy. It may be difficult not to do so. It may be, indeed it is, the case that certain nations have done so. But it is beyond the power of any historian or political scientist to say that we must all behave in the same way, or that what has been must be. On the contrary the outcome of such a struggle will be deeply affected by the past of the particular nation in question, in the same way as the reaction of children to fire is profoundly influenced by the experience of the individual child. One nation may have used force to settle its internal disputes and learned by experience to dislike the consequences. Such an historical fact is equal in importance to any other cause in deciding the outcome of any crisis of change subsequently faced by that group of human beings.

It is therefore impossible to prophesy with certainty the reaction of individual human beings or societies to the same events. They will differ from individual to individual, and from group to group, and from time to time, according to the lessons that have been learnt by the men and women in question. For this reason alone it is never enough to know, as it is in the physical world, the nature of the external conditions in order to foretell the behaviour of human society.

When, in the second place, we remember that as human beings we possess, in all probability, a certain degree of freedom in our choice as well as a capacity to learn from experience, it becomes even more clear why the social sciences must differ from the natural sciences in the degree of certainty their conclusions can reach. As, however, the explanation of what I mean by freedom and its consequences for the social sciences would lead me to raise philosophical problems that would take too long to resolve, I must be content with stating my personal conviction that a certain degree of freedom is a quality of our experience—that we directly know ourselves to be free to turn to right or left, to read a book or close it—and that the problem set to philosophers and scientists is to explain this phenomenon and not to explain it away. We may, of course, exaggerate the extent of our freedom (as the psychologists have shown) or mistake its nature, but no man really doubts its existence in his practical life. If this argument is sound, then it follows that the degree of unpredictability introduced into human behaviour by the ability to learn from experience is greatly increased.

Again it has often been said that the main difference that distinguishes economics from the natural sciences is that economists and other social scientists cannot make use of controlled experiments. They cannot take a nation and submit it to an inflation, or the destruction of property, just to see what happens. While this is perfectly true and certainly deprives social scientists of one of the most powerful and accurate methods of scientific investigation, I do not believe that it is the real explanation of the difference—for two reasons:

1 Controlled experiments (though the best) are not the only method of verification, and it is a method denied to some physical sciences, astronomy for example. Prophecy in space (i.e. foretelling what will be found to be true in some as yet unexplored part of the field) or prophecy in time (i.e. foretelling what will happen in the future) are just as good methods of

verification as that of controlled experiments and are widely used in all sciences. These are freely available to the social sciences.

2 Conditions approximating to those of controlled experiments are often available in the field of the social sciences. This happens when similar societies or social groups pursue different policies or experience different historical events; for example, when France pursued a deflationary, and Germany an inflationary, policy in 1933; or when a group of similar American schools were submitted to different forms of leadership and discipline.

But whatever the method of study available to the social scientist it is impossible to alter the fact that human beings can alter their response to the same external stimuli and so ruin the accuracy of all mechanically logical generalisations and prophecy.

Nor is the explanation to be found in the greater complexity of the social and psychological facts. I doubt if they are more complex. Certainly the problems of astronomy and physics do not appear to be particularly simple, or any less complex than those of human nature.

It is not the method of study, but the nature of the object studied that differentiates the social from the physical sciences.

From all this a number of conclusions follow.

1 The paradox of economics is now explained. It is a science in the sense that it applies the method of science to an important part of social life. And as this is the only method yet discovered whereby a reliable and progressive understanding of any subject can be slowly built up, it is natural that economics should become an important and popular branch of human learning.

On the other hand, since human behaviour is the object of study in this as in all the other social sciences, it is impossible to reach the level of prophetic certainty that is characteristic of physics and chemistry—not because the problems of human nature are more complex and difficult than those of the physical world, but for the deeper reason that causes and consequences are not limited in the same way in the two cases.

2 From this it follows that the future of economics is of a certain kind. Economic studies will progress enormously. Economists will accumulate more and more relevant observa-

tions of fact, and they will invent ever wider and deeper hypotheses to explain them. Many of these theories will be verified over long periods of time and large areas of society. We shall come to understand more and more about the economic life of mankind. But certainty will always escape us, and prediction miss the mark.

Just because men can learn from experience, they can learn from economics itself, and so the subject destroys its own conclusions by its own discoveries. Economists study the trade cycle, discover the laws of its movements and the methods by which recurrent depressions can be prevented. Economic administrators apply these policies and the laws of development previously established are themselves changed in a way that no knowledge of physics can alter the "laws of nature". Economists must therefore remain content with less spectacular achievements and the public must learn what to expect—a continually changing body of doctrine but a steadily increasing power to control economic processes. This is not a wholly discouraging prospect.

3 One lesson for economists is, however, of outstanding importance. They must realise that they are studying human behaviour and not the formulae of logic and mathematics. Formulae and equations have their place in making thought precise and quantitative, but they are never a substitute for the close observation of the object studied—in this case the way in which men and women behave in certain of their social relationships. Human beings, unlike stones and electricity, feel and think, love and hate, imagine and conceive, judge and act.

All these attributes of human nature are at the centre, and not at the circumference, of the problem. Hence, scientific economists must master many subjects other than their own and incorporate into the body of their subject the findings of historians, sociologists and, above all, psychologists. In the last forty years the scientific method has invaded the last citadel of ignorance—the formation of human character—with remarkable and revolutionary results. It is this new knowledge that is most needed by the economics of the future.

Economics and the Other Social Sciences

So far we have considered the problems that are common to economics and to other social sciences. We must now turn briefly to the question—how is economics related to these other subjects?

First, the central subject of economics is a particular, and very important, human and social problem, that of poverty.

Most of the great group of sciences are concerned with one of the great ills to which mankind is heir. The physical sciences—physics, chemistry, meteorology, engineering—arise from the hard fact that the material world in which we live is not immediately subject to our will. We cannot raise coal from below the earth, or make roads across its surface, or clear the fogs away by merely wishing or willing that these things should be done. The only method by which we have learned a partial mastery of the physical universe is by the scientific study of it. In the same way, we cannot prevent potato blight, or cure the human diseases of pneumonia and tuberculosis, by deciding that these things are evil. It is the biological sciences, like botany, physiology, medicine and biochemistry, that have made it possible for our wishes concerning those evils to become realisable in fact. I do not say that this is the sole cause of, or reason for, the growth of science—science is the product of the fundamental instinct of curiosity—but these are the consequences of it.

Now, economics is concerned with the terrible evil of poverty. We find ourselves living in a world in which there is not enough to go round. If income were equally distributed in Britain, for example, it would not provide more than £8–£10 a week for the representative family of four or five persons. For the world as a whole the figures are a mere fraction of this sum. In India and China, containing half the human race, the comparable figure is about one tenth of it—i.e. 16s. to £1 a week for a family of four or five.

Nor is this world-wide condition of fearful shortage traceable to unfair distribution or periodical unemployment. It is perfectly true that income and property are unequally divided, that there are periods of heavy unemployment, and that these are great and remediable evils. But they are not the main cause of poverty. If the product of industry were to be divided with exact arithmetical equality and maintained always at 100 per cent of capacity, these figures would not be appreciably altered. Indeed, these two assumptions are made in calculating the figures.

No. The cause lies deeper than this and is harder to cure. It arises from a shortage in the means of production throughout the world. There is just not enough fertile land, or ploughs, or mining machinery, or rolling stock, or electricity generating plant, or manual skill, or technical knowledge to raise output to the point at which the standard of living of all mankind could be twice or three times as high as it is at present. We do not know enough, and we have not yet acquired the capital or the trained labour force, to make such an increase in output possible.

We are thus brought back to where this book began. Poverty and shortage infest human life. Economics is the application of the scientific method to the study of why this is so and what can be done about it. Two problems clearly arise at once. How can the shortage of productive resources be overcome? How, in the meantime, should our existing resources be distributed between commodities and services?

The answer to the first problem leads the economist on to consider the problems of production—of increasing knowledge, of accumulating capital, of maintaining full employment, of providing the best incentives, of running the monetary system efficiently and of organising foreign trade. The second question leads on to a consideration of what people want (the theory of demand), the measurement of prices and costs (the theory of value), the distribution of wealth, the movement of labour and capital from industry to industry and occupation to occupation, and the planning of economic activity as a whole. These have all been recurrent themes throughout this book.

Finally, it is necessary to realise that these questions cannot be wholly separated from one another. A society has to solve its economic problems by a set of habits and relationships (social institutions) that cover all its economic life at one and the same time. The capitalist system relies, for example, upon the institution of private property for the organisation of its industries, the provision of its money, the development of its foreign trade, and the accumulation of its capital, all in one fell swoop. It used the habit of acquisitiveness to provide the main incentive for every type of labour and the movement of all its resources. And these economic arrangements must fit into, and are deeply influenced by, the still wider political, social, and psychological habits of the national societies in which they are used. The economic system is, in short, a *system* and can be considered only as a working whole, just as a car or a human being cannot be treated as a mere list of its parts or organs. The significance of the wheels and carburettor and magneto, or of the eyes and the hands and feet, can only be understood in the relations they bear to one another and the working unity of life that arises out of them.

Secondly, it follows from what I have just said that economics should be related to the other social studies—history, law, politics, anthropology, and above all psychology—in a particular way. They should be so intimately joined to one another that they lose, in the long run, their separateness.

Economists are concerned with the economic aspect of human life, politicians with the political aspect, lawyers with the legal aspect and social psychologists with the psychological aspect of social affairs. Now, all these aspects are not really separate from one another. They cannot, in truth, be separated at all. Human beings are not divided up into such watertight compartments. A man is not merely an economic machine or a political animal or a legal unit; nor is he any one of these at any single point of time. He is all these things at one and the same time and all the time. He thinks and eats and lives his life in every one of these fields at once. His work as an industrial "factor of production" is deeply influenced by his heredity, his education, his political opinions and his emotional make-up. His individual behaviour and, to an even greater extent, the behaviour of the social group to which he belongs, are determined by all these forces at the same time. To study one of them in isolation from the rest is unreal.

This is not a theoretical argument, but an immediately practical problem in the conduct of any piece of social research. Let me quote two examples chosen at random from the economic field.

One of the central questions of economics is that of incentives. By what methods can men and women be persuaded to give their best energies and attention to their work? The level of output and, therefore, the standard of living will be deeply influenced by the effectiveness of the methods chosen. Yet it is immediately apparent to anyone who has tried to work on the subject that economics alone cannot yield the full answer; nor can any one of the existing social sciences by itself. Each is essential and none can be left out. The economic historian is needed to describe the various inducements that have been tried in the past and the attitude of the working people to them. The economist alone can describe the social consequences of raising wages or relating them to output or changing costs. The contributions of the industrial psychologist and the personnel manager are fundamental, since it is part of their everyday jobs to deal with just such problems. Even the politician and the social psychologist have studied the relation between opinion and emotion on the one hand, and productivity on the other. No realistic study of the problem can be made without the co-operation of all these specialists.

Again—and in quite a separate field—the subject of capital accumulation and the saving habits of the people is of central importance. There can be no economic and industrial progress without it. How can societies save? What are the consequences of their saving? How much ought they to save? All these questions are of prime importance.

The historian must tell us how societies have saved in the past and what consequences followed from their doing so. The economist must describe the mechanisms of capital accumulation in our present society and the probable effects of various rates of saving upon the economic life of the nation. The lawyer must tell us about the institution of property and the psychologist must throw light upon the emotional significance of acquiring it. All these have something to say that is more than interesting—something without which the study is incomplete and the conclusions are unreliable.

It follows from all this that the future of economic science must lie in bringing all these separate special studies together. The economist must co-operate with the accountant, with the historian, with the psychologist, to study some part of social reality in all its complexity. The existing social sciences, and certainly economics, can no longer stand alone. Co-operative research is essential.

I do not mean by this that all economists must be working with other social scientists all the time. That would be an intolerable limitation upon the freedom of their mind and work. Many workers in the economic field will wish to remain free and develop the subject independently. And the same will be true of many historians, lawyers, statisticians and psychologists. But if we are to learn more about the societies in which we live, and if these subjects are to be saved from the sterility of excessive abstraction, a number of specialists must overlap the narrow boundaries of their own subjects and work together on the common problems—the real questions—that now escape between their separate studies. In this, as in many fields of human activity, we must live and work together or hang separately.

Conclusion

Economics, then, is the application of the scientific method to the study of poverty, of the problems raised by the fact that the resources at the disposal of human societies are quite insufficient to provide us with all the goods and services we should like to have. The results obtained by economists will always fall short of the certainty and universality of the physical sciences because human beings, who make up these societies, possess the power of learning from experience and of choosing between the objects of their activity. They must emancipate themselves from the certainty that the same causes will produce the same results, and so greatly restrict the extent to which any accurate prophecies can be made about their future behaviour.

Nevertheless, economics is a valuable and essential study. No one has yet discovered any method, other than that of science, for bringing the physical world under partial control. There is no rival to the same method for studying the problems of society. If we are to master the evils of poverty and unemployment, of injustice, neurosis and war, we must now look first to the social scientists. And since we live in a democracy in which the pace of public policy is ultimately decided by the extent of public understanding and the furniture of men's minds, it is essential that we should all do our best to master the conclusions that are slowly established. That is the main purpose of writing and reading this book.

METHODS OF RESEARCH

In this Paper I seek to apply the general conclusions of the previous Paper on "The Nature of Economics" to one particular matter—the future of economic research. It contains a plea for co-operation between economists and other specialists etc. in the social sciences—historians, lawyers, politicians, sociologists and psychologists.

> "We find, too, that those who are engaged in metaphysical pursuits are far from being able to agree among themselves, but that, on the contrary, this science appears to furnish an arena specially adapted for the display of skill or the exercise of strength in mock contests—a field in which no combatant ever yet succeeded in gaining an inch of ground, in which, at least, no victory was ever yet crowned with permanent possession."—*Kant.*[1]

THERE is, broadly speaking, no serious controversy over the theory of method in this country. There is a difference of emphasis. There is an irritation about phrases. But almost all students of society are in perfect agreement that any exclusive concentration upon observation or reason, theory or application, is mistaken. The most outspoken champions of pure logic—such as Professor Robbins[2]—would be the last to decry the study of economic practice. To do so would be to confine our reflections entirely to circular reasoning. Nor would the advocates of empirical studies—such as Sir William Beveridge[3] or Mrs. Wootton[4]—deny themselves the aid of reason and hypothesis. No science has ever proceeded without the use of pure reason. To deny the necessity of it to science would involve, among other things, a denial of the use of mathematics as an integral part of physics. We can add nothing to Kant's judgment:

[1] Preface to the Second Edition of the *Critique of Pure Reason*, Meiklejohn's translation.
[2] *Nature and Significance of Economic Science*. 2nd Edition. Cf. Chapter IV, *passim*.
[3] *The Place of the Social Sciences in Human Knowledge*, Politica, 1937.
[4] *Lament for Economics*, Chapter III.

Problems of Economic Planning

"Thoughts without content are void; intuitions without conceptions, blind."[1]

Only by the union of reason with observation can anything new be discovered. Surely this is obvious? Surely no one now denies it?

If, then, we are in agreement about what we ought to be doing, why is there so much dissatisfaction within and without the circle of technical economists? Few would deny that such a dissatisfaction exists. We seem to achieve so little by way of a fruitful *union* between the two activities of thinking and observing. And if we do not make this judgment on the results of our efforts, the external observers of our subject make it.

It is the purpose of this article to inquire why this is so. It is the argument of this article that we fail, in so far as we fail, in the first place because we make no effort to bring theory and observation together in any synthesis of our own, and in the second place because we do not co-operate sufficiently with other specialists external to the field of economics. As I shall argue, this is not in the least to decry any work that is now being done. It is only to ask for something else to be done as well. Part I of this article is concerned with the first of these needs, and Part II with the second requirement.

I

2 If we examine the actual output of current literature—in the journals and from the publishers—we shall find an extraordinary divorce between theorising and observation. It is not that either type of work is being neglected, but that each type is pursued by different people, on different subjects, in almost complete isolation from one another.

Excellent work is poured out continuously in both fields of theoretical and applied economics. The journals and the publications of economists are full of both. Our pure theory is developing at a bewildering pace into an unintelligible thicket of complex variables and mathematical symbols. At the same time our knowledge of agricultural marketing boards and the mobility of labour and the administration of unemployment

[1]Kant, *Critique of Pure Reason*. "Transcendental Logic: Of Logic in General." Meiklejohn's translation.

insurance grows—voluminously. But somehow the union between the two, the verification of old, the emergence of new, hypotheses is mysteriously and disastrously missing. It is difficult to think of an important work of verification undertaken in recent years.[1]

In fact, economists are doing two things, and doing them well, but doing them separately. In the first place, they are proceeding apace with the construction of systematic theorems in pure logic based upon assumptions. We all know the articles that begin "I shall, in the course of this article (or chapter or book), *assume* that there are three men producing two commodities with two factors of production under conditions of perfect foresight." We most of us have frequently written such essays in pure logic. Here are a few examples from recent literature:

"We shall *assume* a community which is wholly engaged in the production of a single homogeneous good, which we shall call Bread . . . *assume* perfect competition in the market for loans, and consequently in the market for bread" (J. R. Hicks, *Economic Journal*, Sept. 1935).

"To simplify the problem still further, let us *assume* in the first instance that there are no contracts enduring for longer than the average period of transaction velocity . . ." (E. F. M. Durbin, *The Problem of Credit Policy*, p. 45).

"*Let us suppose*, for example, a community where the sole product, and also (by a stretch of imagination!) the only finished commodity which its inhabitants buy consists of boots" (M. Dobb, *Political Economy and Capitalism*, p. 215).

In all these cases both the author and the reader know that the premise of the argument is not only insufficient and un-

[1]Of course, this statement is not strictly true. There is a small stream of studies that do attempt a process of testing and verification. Recent examples of this kind of thing are Mr. Whale's article "The Working of the Pre-War Gold Standard", *Economica*, 1937, the works of Messrs. Fowler and Coase on the cycle of pig production and much of Mr. Colin Clark's statistical work. But the quantity of such work is small in comparison with the output of the other two types of publication, and economists do not appear to recognise that this is the only part of their output that follows the traditional methods of scientific inquiry. A mathematician is not a physicist, much less an engineer. An econometrician is not an economist, much less a political economist.

Of course there are classical works in this field—Viner's *Balance of Canadian International Indebtedness*, Bresciani-Turroni's *The Economics of Inflation* and the *Inductive Verification of the Theory of International Payments*, and Wesley Mitchell's early work upon the statistics of the Trade Cycle. But most of this work is noticeably in the past. As I shall argue before this article is finished, the output of work is greatly influenced by intellectual fashions.

realistic, but that it is even not true. It is scarcely surprising that theories based upon such hypotheses should remain out of touch with observation and below the level of verification.

This is not, let me repeat, to decry these studies in the very least. They are perfectly necessary. They correspond to the work of the mathematician in the service of physics. They advance our understanding and complete the circle of our logic. But they do not produce in themselves knowledge of reality. Nor are they the full work of science. The mathematician is not the physicist.

On the other hand, we have an immense outpouring of statistics about everything, from bank clearings to the consumption of cosmetics, and careful factual studies of every piece of legislation and economic practice from the recovery measures of President Roosevelt to the currency legislation of the Mauritius. Here are a few titles chosen at random from recent journals:

"Recent Changes in the Physical Output of Arable Farms."
"Return to Capital in the Witwatersrand Gold Industry, 1887–1932."
"The United States Social Security Act."
"Cotton Indices."
"Labour Mobility in the Steel Industry."
"The Profits of Professional Speculators."

Now, some economists think they have refuted the charge that economists as a class are responsible for too much abstract theory when they point to the existence and volume of this empirical work. But they have done no such thing, because, broadly speaking, there is no relationship whatever between this empirical work and the concurrent output of theoretical logic. These factual studies are not made to illuminate, verify or prove some general hypothesis—but simply to establish the facts. "Thoughts without content—blind intuitions."

Again, this is not to depreciate these studies in the slightest. They are absolutely essential to the progress of our knowledge. We must establish the facts. We must know what happens. No science can proceed without data. On the other hand, no science exists unless it proceeds beyond, or through the data, to hypothesis and understanding. It is not what we do, but what we do not do, that makes us weak. We are guilty of sins of omission, rather than commission.

The consequences of this unnatural divorce between theory and fact are disastrous. To begin with, it determines our ridiculous attitude to evidence. As economists we feel satisfied that we have done our work when we have advanced a new theory that is logically consistent but to support which we have offered no single jot or tittle of evidence. The neglect of evidence, indeed the contempt for evidence, felt by economists is simply extraordinary. What on earth is the good of a new theory for whose truth no evidence is offered? How are conflicts between contradictory theories ever to be resolved apart from an appeal to new facts? Growing complexity and growing conflict must be the result—and is the result—as the present state of monetary and trade-cycle theory demonstrates. [1]

Nor does the method of "successive approximation" (as some people [2] call it) offer any substantial hope. It is perfectly true that when the economic logician goes on from the assumption of barter to the assumption of money, or from the assumption of one commodity to the assumption of many, he is moving one step nearer to reality in each case. But without an appeal to evidence he never reaches it. The possible determinants are so many, their possible quantitative relationships so varied, that an end to the process of successive approximation is never made. Unless there is some method of discovering what *in fact* are the quantitatively important variables, progress towards a scientific hypothesis is largely illusory.

An excellent example of this fact is the recent work upon "expectations". Economists began to realise a few years ago that decisions in the real world may be governed, and in some cases must be governed, just as much by the expectations of future prices as by the knowledge of past and present prices. Hence we are now grafting on to the complex body of the theory of value another set of *assumptions*—about the possible forms such expectations may take. This is plainly a step towards reality— in that sense an "advance in", or a "contribution to", our subject. Yet nothing of prophetic or scientific value is added to

---

[1] Cf. Mr. Keynes' *General Theory of Employment, Interest and Money*, Mr. Harrod's *The Trade Cycle*, and my own *Problem of Credit Policy* without a statistic of any importance between them. Of course it is not necessary to point out that Mr. Keynes, at least, has done a great deal of brilliant verificatory work, particularly in Vol. II of his *Treatise on Money*.

[2] Cf. review of Mr. Harrod's *The Trade Cycle* in *Economica* for 1937.

economics if wherever we used to say "price" we now say "expected price". The possible ways in which expectation may be related to knowledge, and the possible sizes of all these relationships, are so immense in number that until we have discovered evidence that throws light upon the actual relationship of these two states of mind (knowledge of, and expectation about, economic quantities), we are not really any nearer to the formulation of hypotheses, even though we have introduced another variable.

On the other hand, it is no use whatever, as I have already argued, to turn in despair to the mere accumulation of information—to the "discovery of the facts". Facts do not speak for themselves. It is only by analysis, comparison, hypothesis and prophecy that they can be made to speak at all. The piling up of undigested information, the compiling of vast statistical tables, the detailed recording of events in time, create the same illusion of discovery for the compiler and the recorder as do the equations for the logician. But it is equally an illusion. Unless there are comparisons to suggest causes, and hypotheses to make prophecies, however humble, the facts remain what Kant called them "blind intuitions".[1]

It is because of the separation of elements that should be united that we have, as economists and social scientists, so little sense of progress, so little proof and disproof, such deep and humiliating disagreements. As long as the two activities of the mind, each essential in itself, are not joined in fruitful union, we shall make little progress. It is only from that difficult embrace that positive economic or social science can spring.

3 But is such a positive social science in any way possible? I must turn aside from my main task for a moment to answer this question, because I feel sure that many economists are prevented from pursuing the methods of science because they believe that the end in view is inherently unattainable. Now, there are perfectly good reasons for supposing that the prophetic power and precision of the physical and biological sciences are for ever denied to the social sciences. But let us be clear exactly why this is so—for a number of false reasons are frequently advanced for supposing it.

[1] For an excellent example of this sort of thing see Schmidt's *German Business Cycles* and in another field of inquiry Mr. Tom Harrisson's *Mass Observation*.

In the *first* place, it is not true that the "complexity of the social problem" is a sound reason for failing to attempt verification. Social scientists appear to assume that the physical and biological worlds are in some sense "simpler" than society. But what earthly reason is there for supposing so? It is perfectly true that we now know more of the real forces determining the form of physical and biological events than we do of those determining social events. But that is precisely because the faculties of observation, comparison, reasoning, prophecy and verification have been used in co-operation to discover the quantitatively important variables in the data of observation. The physical world and the problems of the physical sciences were not "simple" to the sixteenth- and seventeenth-century scientists. On the contrary, they were immensely complex and baffling. The scientists of that time were floundering in the way that we are floundering now, because they had not yet discovered real lines of causal connection. Confusion was bound to reign as long as it was supposed that physiological processes were determined by the compounding of four vital elements, or that the sequence of physical events was determined by the conjunctures of the stars. "Simplicity" merely means "knowledge of the true determinants". It is at least possible that we continue to flounder in the social sciences because we have not yet discovered the important variables.

In the *second* place, the fact that we "cannot make use of the experimental method" is not a sufficient reason to abandon the hope of verification. Astronomy cannot make use of the experimental method. Medical and psychiatric diagnoses cannot make use of the experimental method. Yet none of these sciences is denied the fruits of verification. The truth is that the experimental method is not the solitary, although it is the best, method of verification. The method of comparison is available. By it the common characteristics of diverse instances can be revealed. The method of prognosis or prophecy is available. Inaccurate prophecy will at least disprove wrong hypotheses. The method of "parallel prophecy", or forecasting what will be found to be true in evidence not yet known by the theorist, is available. By all these methods evidence can be discovered, and theories can be tested, without conducting a single experiment upon society.

This is not the place to embark upon a dicussion of the elementary notions of scientific method. We all know what they are. We all know the methods by which the doctor, the business man, the civil servant and the politician proceed—and must proceed. They act upon hypotheses rooted in evidence, whose truth or falsehood is revealed only in the outcome of action based upon them. We all know what we mean by "offering evidence" that a theory is true or false. The only purpose of this article is to apply to the existing social studies the principle that the traditional method of science lies in establishing theories out of evidence and by the verification of hypotheses; and to assert that important methods of verification are open to us.

4 Now, this is not to say that there are no good reasons for believing that the fruits of our scientific labours will always be different in kind from those of the physical and biological sciences. That is because of the nature of the object we study— the behaviour of mankind. [1] Whether or not men possess a *free will*—and few serious thinkers deny the existence of some range of personal choice—they plainly possess the power to learn from experience. The presence of this faculty has been experimentally demonstrated in all the higher mammals. The consequences for scientific study are immense. Accurate prophecy becomes impossible. The essential condition of prophecy in the physical sciences is absent. Similar observable conditions will not necessarily produce similar results. Behaviour is determined not only by objective conditions, but also by the internal accumulation of memory and knowledge. Individuals will not always react in the same way to the same stimuli—nor will societies. And if to this unquestionable faculty of man be added the probability of freedom, accurate foresight becomes inherently impossible.

And yet, when this has been said, nothing has been said. The interesting hypothesis for science is not the hypothesis of freedom, but the hypothesis of determinism—not because we are ignorant of the other element in man's nature, or unaware of the ultimate limits it sets to our studies, but because it is the

[1]For an illuminating discussion of this problem see John MacMurray's *Interpreting the Universe*. In this book Prof. MacMurray discusses the problems raised for science by the division of the observed and comprehended world into three broad forms or orders of being—inanimate matter, living matter and personality.

only fruitful hypothesis, because in every field in which it has been tried the hypothesis of determinism has so far yielded light.

5 The task of the social scientist is therefore the same in all essential principles as that of the natural scientist—to apply logical processes to the data of observation and to attempt the verification of hypotheses upon the assumption of the continuity, and the determination by general laws, of all events. How can that be done?

Within the existing field of economics the first answer is obvious—to give up writing books without theories and books without evidence. Until we are all concerned to prove the theories we hold by an appeal to the facts, and to withdraw our interest from fields in which disputes can never be resolved, we shall proceed but slowly to agreement in the light of knowledge. We shall continue to tilt against each other in the "arena" that Kant describes as "specially adapted for the display of skill . . . in mock contests . . . a field in which no combatant ever yet succeeded in gaining an inch of ground, in which . . . no victory was ever yet crowned with permanent possession".

Nor is there any good reason for believing that this change is difficult to make. The chief interests of economists are so much a matter of fashion. In the last ten years there has been an immense increase in the interest in abstract theory—especially among younger economists.[1] It would only require a similar change in fashion to bring evidence, and the search for proof, back to the front of the stage—to the immense improvement in the health of our studies. That would carry us a long way. But it would not carry us quite far enough, and I wish in the second part of this article to offer a few reflections on a further question of method in research.

II

6 There is, I have argued, no real disagreement amongst us about the *theory* of method. The only interesting problem is that of the technique of research. How are hypotheses to be made, how are they to be verified, how is agreement to be reached? I have already discussed one suggestion—that we should restore evidence to its central position in our work.

[1] I must confess to having been deeply influenced by this fashion myself.

But there is another problem to which we must now turn—that of our relations with other social studies. To do this it is necessary to make another adverse criticism of the present state of the social sciences. They do not, as it seems to me, achieve a proper sub-division of the field of a study.

Sub-division is, of course, desirable and inevitable. The natural sciences would have got nowhere if all scientists had studied the whole of the natural world. The social sciences would have got nowhere if we had all studied the whole of society. But the fact remains that, unlike the natural sciences, our sub-divisions are largely (though not entirely) *abstractions from* reality rather than *sections of* reality.

Botany is a study of a group of organisms—plants. Zoology is a study of a different group of organisms—animals. Colloidal chemistry is a study of a group of substances—colloids. Crystallography is a study of a group of objects—crystals. In all these cases the objects of study are real and independent objects and groups. They are not aspects of something complex. They are real things. But are most of our subjects so distinguished? Are they not mostly aspects of, abstractions from, social reality? Is economics not a study of the *economic aspect* of social behaviour? Is the academic subject of law not a study of the *legal aspects* of social behaviour? Is political history not a study of the *political aspects* of general history? And economic history a study of the *economic aspects* of general history? That is to say, our sub-divisions turn, once more, upon the definition of terms: economic, legal, political—and not upon sub-divisions inhering in the objects of study.

And of course most social scientists recognise this. Even if we accept Prof. Robbins' definition of the subject-matter of our present economics as "the study of the behaviour of men in their attempt to dispose scarce resources between alternative uses", neither Prof. Robbins nor any other economist would deny that such behaviour is influenced by political ideas, laws and historical traditions. Lawyers increasingly recognise that law and the development of law is influenced by "economic" and "political" forces. The course of "political" history cannot seriously be supposed to be independent of "economic" events —and so forth. These considerations should force us to ask whether our present subjects do correspond to any real divisions in our object of study. Reality may escape between our "aspects" of it.

7 But, it may well be asked, what things in society are more real than these "aspects" of social behaviour to the study of which we now devote our energies? I think certain things have more independent existence than our conceptions of "economic behaviour" or "legal acts". I think definite periods of history possess more independent reality—in this case, independence in time. I think primitive societies, or separate urban communities, possess more independence—independence in space. I think social institutions like property; or patterns of social behaviour like the distribution of authority; or repeated sequences of events in time, like trade cycles; all possess more real existence than our general "aspects". They are parts of real social behaviour that can at least be observed in their entirety.

But the moment we specify any more concrete problem of this kind we are faced by the terrible dilemma of our present methods of study. Supposing that we wanted to study any one of these true sub-divisions—a small urban community, for example, or property, or war, or trade cycles—then all our present subjects, or most of them, are relevant to such a study just because they consist in the abstraction of essential elements present in almost all social behaviour. Take a few random examples:

(*a*) Suppose we wished to understand the legal institution of *property*; its nature, origin, present significance and probable future. How many of our existing subjects can, indeed should, contribute to our study? Almost all. Without the aid of law we cannot understand what the institution is. Without general history we cannot say how it came into existence or what are the forces likely to change it. Without economics we cannot understand its consequences. Many of its implications are brought to light by psychology. General sociology and anthropology have an important contribution to offer. Without the aid of all or most of these existing subjects we cannot say that we are studying this institution in its real social existence, or putting ourselves in a position to make prophecies about its future.

(*b*) Or suppose that we wished to study *war*—a concrete,

tragically concrete, social phenomenon. History is essential. Psychology is essential. Anthropology is essential. Economics and general sociology have valuable contributions to make.

(*c*) And the same is true of many of the subjects that are now regarded as primarily economic. *Trade cycles* are a good example. To study them as concrete social phenomena, subjects other than economic theory and statistics are relevant. If we are to discover their origin, we must look to economic history. If we are to understand their effects, we must turn to political and social history. Economists are increasingly using terms like "expectation" and "confidence" that cry out for psychological investigation. The existing subject of politics has much to contribute to an understanding of future policy. Without all these aids we are in no position to construct hypotheses or analyse the existing evidence.

Thus it would seem that the study of reality cuts across, or rather embraces, all our existing specialisms. United we might stand. Divided we certainly fall. How are we, then, to stand together?

There is one superficially attractive way in which I very much doubt if it is possible to proceed very far. That is by the creation of specialists and specialisms in more concrete subjects of study. It might appear that we should do best to create research posts for the study of property, or war, or trade cycles. But is this really a wise procedure? Is the person paid to carry out this work really in a position to do it? Think of the task that faces him—or her? He must keep pace with the most recent developments of all the subjects that are relevant to the study of the particular problem allotted to him. The student of war must keep pace with the historical material, the anthropological evidence, with the developments of modern psychology, and economics and general sociology. The task is gigantic. Most of us find it difficult to keep pace with the work published in one of the main sub-divisions of economics—such as monetary and trade-cycle theory—without being asked to undertake four or five such subjects at once. It seems scarcely possible that it should be done.

Is there, then, no practicable procedure? Must we resign ourselves to our separate and abstract researches or scrap the whole framework of our present subjects and start again from the beginning? I hardly think either drastic alternative is necessary.

8 I would suggest, very tentatively, that much the most fruitful line of advance must lie in exploring further the possibilities of co-operation between existing specialists.

Let me explain at once that I am not advocating vast and elaborate schemes of "co-operative research". We all know of complicated and pretentious institutions and projects for research that cost millions of dollars and produce no substantial results whatever. White elephants in labour to produce platitudinous mice. This was, and is, largely because the schemes are ill conceived, insufficiently considered and infected from the beginning with administrative elephantiasis and intellectual paralysis. But it does not follow that because this sort of thing has been done badly it cannot in any circumstances be done well. If bad beginnings damned a procedure, modern surgery would never have developed.

Nor am I suggesting for one moment that we can ever dispense with individual research. It would be a horrible proposal to condemn us all to compulsory intellectual matrimony. Such unions would be foredoomed to sterility. We must all of us be free for part of our time, and some of us free for all of our time, to continue a solitary search for truth.

But until we have found some real determinants of social behaviour, and as long as the separate specialisms are rushing away from each other at such a break-neck speed, some kind of intellectual co-operation is vitally necessary. The need is not met by "team research" of the ordinary kind. Of course team-work is an invaluable method of study for certain problems. Social surveys, market researches, wide empirical studies of all kinds, can only proceed by using this technique. Yet, unless the teams are composed of *different* specialists, the central problems of our subjects cannot be resolved. Until the economist, the lawyer, the historian and the psychologist shall co-operate in some way in the study of property, property as a concrete social phenomenon will not be studied.

9 How should different specialists co-operate?

The space at my disposal does not enable me to discuss the answer to this question in any detail. Nor, perhaps, is it worth doing so at the present time. The purpose of this article will have been more than served if I have succeeded in convincing a fraction of its readers that the principle of co-operation is a sound one. Given the principle—we can only discover the best techniques for giving effect to it by practical experience in co-operation.

It is, however, perhaps worth saying a word or two on the general principles of technique. There are obviously a number of methods of co-operation available: committees of specialists on concrete problems with or without paid secretaries; joint seminars, discussion groups or courses of lectures; research students working under two or more senior advisers; the appointment of lawyers to economics departments and psychologists to history departments; the continuous co-operation over long periods of small groups of friends who study particular subjects. Whatever the methods, there are, I believe, certain essential conditions for success:

(*a*) That the projects should be modest at the beginning. Attempts at co-operation in the past have been vitiated by their size and ambition. Better that an economist and a lawyer should study the incidence of rates than that six full-time specialists should announce their intention to "reveal the institutional basis of modern society". Best of all that manageable tasks of real importance should be discovered and attacked.

(*b*) That the most fruitful work is likely to come from small groups of specialists who know and trust one another and who meet over long periods of time in the normal course of their working lives. It is therefore especially in large institutions already specialising in the social sciences that co-operative work could most fruitfully be attempted.

(*c*) That it is difficult to believe that much work of this kind can be done unless it is paid for. If we are all employed to teach the existing specialisms or to research in them it is unlikely that much of our time can be spared for other tasks. Of course, a little work can be done on a voluntary basis. But the pressure to keep pace with the developments of the central subject of our employment will reserve the best of our work for our present abstractions. It is only if part of the obligations of somebody's regular job consists in such labour that much of it will be done.

In conclusion I should like to say that it would be most interesting to know if there are any other economists who have felt the need for wider co-operation in the social sciences, and to discover from them if they have made any progress towards the solution of the exceedingly difficult problems of method.

ECONOMISTS AND THE FUTURE
FUNCTIONS OF THE STATE

In 1943 I tried to meet the charge that economists never agree about anything by attempting to demonstrate that they had a large number of common opinions about one of the most controversial subjects of our time —the proper function of the State in the field of economic life.

IT is a commonplace that the State has been extending the control of economic activities in this country ever since the Great Depression and that this development has been greatly accelerated by the requirements of total war.

Have we economists, as such, anything to say in agreement with one another about this change—about the future relations of State and industry? Has "economic science" any "lessons" to teach the general public? Or has the dogmatism of the nineteenth century wholly disappeared into a chaotic welter of conflicting opinions?—robbing economics and economists of all "scientific" authority?

The layman certainly thinks so and a considerable number of economists would agree with him. Yet I am not convinced that the familiar appearance of universal disagreement represents the whole reality of the matter, and in this article I wish to explore the directions in which agreement between economists might be found.

2 It is of considerable importance for both economists and the public to know whether economists have anything to say, as economists, about economic problems. It is important for economists because they can scarcely expect to influence economic policy unless they are agreed about something, and it is important for the public because they certainly need, and can reasonably ask for, scientific guidance from the body of specialists whom they pay to study these matters. It is a poor subject indeed if it produces nothing but disputes and acrimony.

Economists and the Future Functions of the State

If doctors could agree about nothing, if one doctor recommended the treatment of influenza by keeping the patient warm in bed and another by forcing him into a cold bath, and if both doctors went out of their way to accuse each other publicly of vice and stupidity it would scarcely be surprising if the layman refused to listen to either of them and came to the conclusion that the study of medicine was a waste of time and money. Economists have come perilously near to discrediting themselves in this way, but I do not believe that it was or is necessary for them to do so. [1]

2 I am not, of course, unaware of the profound philosophical obstacles that lie in the way of economists reaching agreement about economic policy. Economists, like mathematicians, have no choice but to agree, in the long run, about economic theory. When the assumptions upon which trains of a prior reasoning are based have been clarified the conclusions are inescapable—they possess the necessity of logic, no more and no less. But in recommending policy two further sources of reasonable difference at once appear. In the first place economists may make differing judgments of moral value and therefore come to hold opposing views on the objects of policy (e.g. on the desirability of equality in distribution or the correct relationship between wages and productivity); and in the second place they may judge social reality differently and therefore expect different results to flow from the commission of certain acts of policy (e.g. they may reasonably differ about the effects of public works on business confidence or of changes in the level of income tax upon the willingness to work and save). It is, therefore, unlikely, to say the least of it, that economists will ever run short of subjects to argue about and there is no danger that we shall easily reach any sterile uniformity.

[1] Economists became discredited in the early thirties through indulging in disputes that became unduly acrimonious. We deprived ourselves, quite unnecessarily, of all influence. And yet the propositions to which all, or very nearly all, economists could have been persuaded to subscribe were, or very soon became, far more important than the scholastic details over which we quarrelled bitterly and, worse still, loudly. Pursuing with passion the by-ways of thought, moved by academic austerity and human vanity, we forgot to state with authority the simpler conclusions that were not in dispute between us. Yet this common doctrine would have brought a flood of light to the harassed politician and public servant. This tragedy of wasted knowledge will be repeated after the war if economists do not give their best energy to stating and enlarging the field of their agreement. The subject is greater than the professor of it. To spread understanding is more fruitful than to win dialectical victory.

Nevertheless, the difficulties are not insurmountable, and indeed, economics does not exist if economists agree about nothing and we are taking money from society on false pretences if we have nothing to say, in common, that is of value to the layman in guiding his decision on economic questions. Nor are we, I shall argue, cursed by any such impotence. We have failed to influence action because we have not in recent years attempted to reach, or publish, agreements among ourselves and not because we have no agreements to publish.[1]

3 To return to my particular question—the future economic activities of the State. At the moment these activities are greatly extended. The Government is the predominant authority in guiding the economic life of the nation. The Treasury collects and spends over 60 per cent of the National Income. It controls all dealings in foreign exchange and the Ministries of Food and Supply possess, between them, a virtual monopoly of foreign trade. The use of all, or almost all, imported and home-produced foodstuffs and raw materials is controlled and rationed. A great variety of prices are fixed by Order in Council and most men and women are subject to some kind of direction. We have taken immense strides towards the creation of a fully planned economy.

A number of these activities will be curtailed as soon as the "transitional period" following the war is over. It is to be hoped and expected that the consumption of services by the Government will be reduced and that of private consumers increased. It is most unlikely that the powers of the Minister of Labour to interfere with the choice of occupation (amounting as they do to a conscription of industrial labour) will be allowed to continue. The direct production of arms by the State will diminish. But most of these new powers and activities will not disappear automatically—except in the purely legal sense that most of them depend upon Emergency Regulations. If they are allowed to cease it will be the result of deliberate decisions. The power to determine the internal level of expenditure, the monopoly of foreign exchange and foreign trade, the purchasing activities of the Ministry of Food and the Ministry of Supply,

---

[1]It has been my good fortune to witness the remarkable consequences of one group, containing economists of very different opinions, making a serious attempt to formulate their common convictions. The attempt was surprisingly successful.

the direction of the railways and the coal industry, and the control of prices, need not pass away with the emergency that brought them into existence, and my question becomes: Should they do so? Do economists think that some or all or none of these new activities ought to be preserved after the war is over?

4 It would be foolish to suggest that there is any appearance of unanimity among us on the central question of principle that is involved—the future relationship between State and industry. Indeed, the views economists have expressed appear to be diametrically opposed to one another; and I must turn to consider them.

There are at least three distinguishable "schools of thought".[1]

First there are those who hold that it will be desirable to contract the economic activities of the State as much as possible and as soon as the economic emergency (as distinct from the war) is over—that public policy must be based upon the assumption that private initiative is preferable to control by the State.

This is a traditional line of thought, but in the writings of the more careful members of the "Neo-Classical" School it is

[1] I should perhaps explain that my classification of economists into three "schools of thought" is largely an expository device. There is, of course, every variety of opinion and shade of emphasis among economists and the lines of division are crossed and blurred by numberless individual variations. There is, nevertheless, some guidance to be derived from a rough grouping. If names are of any value it would be possible to attach that of Professor Hutt to the first group, Mr. H. D. Dickinson to the second group, and possibly Lord Keynes to the third—but I have not examined the views or quoted from the writings of any particular members of either group, and the economists whose names I have quoted will, I hope, forgive me if I have inadvertently misrepresented them by using their distinguished names as labels.

I should also add that I have not considered the views (at least in this article) of the small minority of economists who occupy positions on the extreme Right and on the extreme Left of the central body of opinion classified here. There are economists who believe in the maintenance of restrictive control—bilateral clearing agreements, the quantitative limitation of imports, and the maintenance of schemes for restricting primary production. At the other extreme there are those who believe in the desirability of a swift and revolutionary creation of a fully planned economy on the Russian model. I have not dealt with these extreme "schools of thought", because they contain, between them, such a tiny number of professional economists; and because I believe that in the field of economic policy, as in all other parts of our national life, extreme opinion is of little practical (though of much theoretical) interest. The climate of our society is not favourable to its growth. I do not, of course, mean by this that truth is necessarily to be found in common opinion or best pursued in the company of a crowd. Nevertheless the minority of economists subscribing to either the strict Conservative or Communist "school of thought" is too small to take any large place in a study primarily concerned to explore the grounds of agreement.

now far removed from the earlier doctrines of *laisser faire*—complete inactivity on the part of the State. They no longer suggest that there is a "natural" economic order independent of law, politics and opinion or that the capitalist system is less the conscious creation of the State than any other set of economic arrangements. They hold, on the contrary, that the State must be more active if competitive capitalism is to survive, but it must be active in a certain way. It must make itself the vigilant and persistent enemy of monopoly and combinations. It must experiment with subtle methods of "trust-busting" and deliberately promote equality of opportunity and individual initiative.

The desirability of preserving private enterprise, competition and property is defended by two persuasive arguments. These are:

(*a*) Men tend to act in their own interest. When they combine together into groups—particularly groups of producers—the interests of the individuals become radically opposed to the common purposes of society. The profit of a monopoly lies in the restriction of output—that of society in enlarged production. The members of a Trade Union can secure higher wages by excluding a minority from work while the common interest demands that all should be employed. The temptation to use the power acquired by "combinations in restraint of trade" is too great to be resisted and Societies stand in constant peril of passing into the paralysing grip of organised minorities. Syndicalism is the enemy.[1]

(*b*) The problem of wise economic administration is that of making constant adjustments, as rapidly as possible, to an immense number of external changes. This is a form of behaviour that cannot be directed from the centre or subjected to a rigid plan. The variables are too many to be related in one mind (or on one Committee) and the conditions have altered before a plan can be made or enforced. It would, those economists feel, be no more wise to subject the infinite variety of economic movement to central direction than to "plan" the movement of the waves in a storm or autumn leaves in a gale. Industrial and commercial administration must be "de-centralised" and the institution of property provides a large, flexible and responsible army of administrators with which to do it.

If these arguments are accepted it follows that the State

[1]The syndicalist minority is not necessarily formed exclusively from one economic or social class. That, according to members of this school of thought, was one of Marx's mistakes. It is certainly true that, in our own day, employers and employed, rentier and wage-earner, have combined together to support restrictive schemes of many kinds.

should be continuously active in securing equality of economic opportunity for all persons at all ages by the positive provision of free education from the elementary school to the university; by making information available through Employment Exchanges, consumer research councils and public reports on the market for new securities; and by guaranteeing to everyone equality before the law. In addition it must preserve the stability of competition by legislating against combinations of all kinds and by protecting individuals from any extreme hardship (due to unemployment, sickness or old age) that would drive them, and the majority of their sympathetic fellow citizens, to repudiate the institutions that caused their suffering. It would be important to see that the level of subsistence obtainable through the charity of the State was not high enough to diminish the willingness to work, but it is logical, as well as humane, for those who believe in capitalism to support the social services that are essential to its continued existence in a democracy.

Nor is it less consistent, though it is less obviously so, for these economists to support, as most of them now do, positive action by the State to offset the depressions of the Trade Cycle through which the capitalist system continuously passes. They would not dispute that wasted resources and unnecessarily low money incomes are offences against reason and that it is therefore imperative for the State to act when no other agent is sufficiently powerful to do so. For the same reason they do not object to the State waging war.

But the State must not embark largely upon manufacture, control competitive industry, or socialise any considerable section of the economy. These economists, therefore, advocate the removal of all restrictive and purely regulative control during the period of "reconstruction"; new legislation against monopolies; and the gradual weakening of the legal privileges now enjoyed by Trade Unions. They are not opposed to gradual improvements in the social services or to policies of public investment and they hope to see, as a result of these reforms, the emergency of a freely moving, rapidly progressing, egalitarian and individualist economy. Theirs is a policy of discriminating constructive de-control.

In sharp contrast stand the views, in the second place, of the economists who believe in the possibility of a flexible planned economy working successfully within the framework of a political democracy—"socialist" (as distinct from communist) economists.

Those writers, who accept the principle that the tastes of consumers should determine the relative outputs of finished commodities, at least within the sector of industry set aside for the satisfaction of private needs, and who therefore wish to preserve the accounting of prices and costs, base their arguments upon two fundamental propositions:

(*a*) They hold that the control, and therefore the conscious planning, of economic activity—the use in this field of the human faculties of observation, induction, reason and foresight—is more efficient, at least in the long run, than the mechanism of instinctive response and the actions of men who are unconscious of the social consequence of their administrative decisions; and that there can be no better case for leaving industrial and financial affairs beyond the direction of the social will than to do the same for education or military affairs or the preservation of public health. To them the hypothesis of human progress is not a myth and the guiding line of that uncertain advance has been, in their view, the gradual extension of understanding and conscious will over the older authority of uncontrollable physical, biological, political and economic events.

(*b*) They must then go on to affirm, since they cannot doubt the strength of vested interests, that there resides somewhere in traditional democracies the power to override the opposition of minorities—as much in the economic as in the political sphere. They do not need to hold that this power is overwhelmingly strong or easily mobilised, that victory will be lightly or quickly gained, but they believe that syndicalism can be finally overcome before the ability of the economy to grow and change has been strangled by the self-protective resistance of minorities that are small or large.

It is obvious that these economists are not concerned to defend restrictionist policies of any sort. Nor do they necessarily wish to remove economic incentives of the ordinary kind (differential earned incomes to induce greater application or efficiency, for example). Nor are they wedded to the doctrine that all industries should be administered in large units. They are not monopolists or arithmetical egalitarians or bureaucrats. They are democratic socialist planners.

They therefore desire to preserve the framework of all the war-time economic activities of the State—apart from the military purchases of the Government and the direction of labour—and to extend them by the purchase of controlling interests in the main industries of the country.

They believe that a number of advantages would flow from the progressive socialisation of industry. In the first place, it seems to them that there is no better, no safer, method of ensuring full employment than to bring a large sector of industrial investment under a unified social control. Any person or Committee that is in a position to decide the level of investment can provide an adequate income within any society and therefore guarantee a sufficiency of work. In the second place, they hold that there is no more likely method to overcome monopoly of all kinds—whether due to technical conditions or the search for profit—and to reap, once more, the fruits of maximum expansion and technical progress. The differences between social and private productivity can be assessed by the practice of more complete accountancy, and the longer foresight of the social mind can be used to guide policy. Finally, they would argue that a more equal, and therefore a more just, distribution of income and property could be safely based upon a socialised industrial system.

At the same time, these economists would be the enemies of centralised administration. They would press for the management of all industries in units of optimal size—where the economies of large-scale production are finally offset by the diseconomies of large-scale oversight—because it would then be possible to preserve the advantages of comparison, experiment and competition in many industries, of which mining and textile manufacture are outstanding examples. Theirs is a programme of social ownership, centralised responsibility, but small-scale administration. And this programme they believe to be compatible with the preservation of political democracy.

6 In the third place, there is, as always in this country, an impressive and influential school of thought that "keeps to the middle of the road". Many economists do not believe in the reality of any dilemma, or "inevitable choice" between a planned and an unplanned economy, between a purified capitalism or a democratic socialism.

They hold that it is absurd to imagine that there is one "right" form of economic control for all periods of history or one "right" type of administration for all industries. It would be as sensible, they think, to suppose that all pretty women had the same shaped face or that all good pictures were painted in one colour. Some industries should be owned and operated by the State, some controlled by it, and others left altogether free. Empiricism is a principle. Each case must be considered on its merits. There must be bold experimentalism and freedom from doctrinaire "systems" of thought.

This sensible avoidance of extremes, they would conclude, is in any case inevitable. When has Britain ever chosen a schematic solution for any problem or failed to find a compromise that confounded all the prophets of conflict? There is no alternative, they would argue, but to discuss each proposal for State intervention on its merits and to develop a "mixed" but virile economy. The important question to answer is not "Are we in favour of a socialist or capitalist economic system?" but "What, precisely, should the State do after the war is over?"

I imagine that most of the members of this school would reply to their own question by stating some programme of this kind:

(*a*) The State should retain its control over the foreign exchanges for a limited period because we are certain to encounter difficulties in restoring our balance of payments after the war and it may be necessary to direct the expenditure of the proceeds from our export sales to the purchase of essential imports. Moreover, they would say, we cannot let any future disturbance in our foreign balance cause unnecessary deflation and unemployment at home. But they would wish to see an early international agreement to offset the movements of the Trade Cycle and to create an international bank with the object of restoring, as soon as possible, an automatic method for equilibrating trade balances.

(*b*) In the second place, they would approve of the Government retaining sufficient power to determine the internal level of monetary expenditure. It is plainly desirable that fluctuations in the outlay of private income should be offset by the balancing activity of the only agent powerful enough to influence the total by a single decision— namely, the central financial authorities of the State. It is a matter of technical detail whether such offsetting should take the form of "public works", or "unbalanced budgets" or less familiar expedients. It is, however, essential for the preservation of stable prosperity, and therefore of economic good sense, that this type of activity on the part of central authorities should be preserved and extended until they are completely effective in preserving full employment.

(*c*) A certain amount of outright industrial socialisation is desirable. Industries that are forced into monopoly for technical reasons—public utilities, electrical supply, railway transport—ought to be owned by the State, since their policy must be controlled in any case, and ownership provides the simplest and most comprehensive method of reaching this goal. In addition, it is conceivable that certain other industries—e.g. aircraft construction—are of such military and international importance that they cannot be safely left in private hands although they are in no danger of becoming monopolies. There will, for these two reasons, be a substantial socialised sector of industry in the economy of the "moderates".

(*d*) Further, in the older industrial economies, certain of the earlier basic industries—coal mining, the manufacture of the coarser textiles, arable farming—are faced with problems of adjustment beyond their unaided capacity to solve. In such cases the pressure of sympathy, the unwillingness to allow large groups of human beings to decay in partial employment and slow financial paralysis, makes the extension of aid to them inevitable. Their appeals will not go unheard. Full ownership is not, however, necessary. It will be sufficient in most cases, in order to help them, to bring the affairs of such industries under general control.[1]

From all this it will follow that a substantial field of industry particularly in the expanding manufacture of new products will be left in the hands of private enterprise. A delicate and eclectic balance will be struck between the integrated and far-seeing activity of the State and the vigorous adaptability of the individual, and small corporation, seeking profit.

Finally, these economists would wish to modify and render tolerable the inequalities of distribution by extending the social provision for education so widely that "equality of opportunity" is everywhere secured and by making charitable aid for the poor continuously more generous—rather than by the abolition of property as an institution. They would point to the strong historical trend towards the widening distribution of small property as a further justification for this decision.

7 It would be idle to pretend that the ground of disagreement among economists is not therefore extensive. But are there no common ideas that can be traced through the diversity of their opinions—no melodies among these discords?

Surely there are four propositions to which all economists

[1]It is not, of course, implied that the aid should be of a restrictionist type. The fundamental problem of such industries is excessive capacity. The object of aid provided by the State should be to secure that inevitable contraction is made as painlessly as possible.

within these groups, or almost all, could be persuaded to subscribe?

In the first place, practically no economist now doubts that something can be done to moderate trade cycle depressions—to reduce the degree of general unemployment. They may differ greatly in their estimates of the extent to which improvement is possible. Some are pessimistic and others optimistic. They are likely to differ about the relative merits of various methods—particularly whether it is more desirable to stimulate investment by public works or consumption by reduced taxation—and they are certain to dispute bitterly about the rival merits of the various terms and theories by which monetary processes can best be described or explained. But to the critical question—should the State pursue policies likely to increase the volume of monetary expenditure during periods of general unemployment?—there is likely to be unanimity in answering yes.

This is a matter of the very greatest importance for the politician, the administrator and the general public. It means that economists do now offer them some hope and a possible cure for the gravest economic disease from which the nation has suffered—and it is important that this point should be widely understood, since the hope can only be realised if we all (politicians, administrators and economists) make a united effort to bring into existence a flexible programme of capital investment. This a difficult administrative task, but it can be done if we approach the problems with a sense of urgency and feel behind us the pressure of the public will. If we succeed we shall banish general or mass unemployment from our midst.

Nor would there be many defections from the harmonious chorus if it were proposed, in the second place, to reinforce measures within one country by international agreements to pursue the policy upon a wider scale and to protect the balance of payments between countries by equilibrating programmes of foreign lending, by the creation of an international bank and by the establishment of agreed rules for the movement of international exchange rates. In the field of financial policy there is a wide, impressive and practical measure of agreement.

In the third place, it is difficult to see that any economist, whatever his school of thought, can be in favour of uncontrolled monopoly or measures aiming merely at the restriction of production. It is, of course, reasonable for economists to argue that no particular harm is done by reducing the output of commodities that are plainly in excessive supply. To diminish, by regulation, the marketing of coal or the growth of wheat at a time when the full output of the industry would keep prices permanently below a profitable level does no more than anticipate the desirable outcome of perfect competition—by bringing output nearer to the point at which price will cover the cost, at current rates of remuneration, of the factors of production. But to leave the matter there is plainly irrational. The disease is not cured. Excessive production is brought about by the attachment of too much labour and capital to the industry in question. In the absence of general unemployment no policy is adequate, and no cure is permanent, that fails to take account of this fact. It is the movement of resources, not the maintenance of prices, that can alone restore a rational equilibrium.

It is surely possible for economists to agree that a great number of measures and policies—quota schemes, tariffs and preferences, subsidies and marketing boards—deserve the criticism that they are merely restrictive impediments to mobility. In some instances it may be reasonable to argue that protective measures are necessary for military reasons.[1] In many more cases the course of events may be so swift that there is no alternative, as a first measure, to organising a restrictive marketing scheme. Politicians are not necessarily short-sighted because they pursue the only practicable policy in a crisis that no one has foreseen. Nor are schemes for orderly marketing, in which large stabilising stocks are held and receipts are equal to costs over a long period of full production, to be condemned, if they are condemned at all, on the ground that they are restrictive. But when all these qualifications have been given due weight there remain marketing arrangements that are purely restrictive in nature—those for cotton in the United States, and for coal in Great Britain—to justify which no

---

[1] In the case of this country, one good shipping yard would seem a safer re-insurance than most tariffs.

strategic argument is valid and in which no provision is made for the necessary outward movement of the human and material resources attached to the industry.

Restrictive policies are pursued for obvious reasons. There is no mystery about it. They are the result of successful pressure by interested minorities and a lack of imagination and administrative vitality on the part of the State. But economists, whether they believe in *laisser faire*, socialist, or mixed economies, have no good reason for defending the over-weening power of producing minorities or excusing the mental and moral inertia of civil servants, politicians and consumers. Economists are the paid "remembrancers" of the public conscience. It is their duty to denounce the specious pleas of monopolist and trade unionist and to summon the lazy citizen to repentance. We are uncomfortable folk, professional prophets, unless we shirk our obligations.

Of course, the real need, in this field, is to discover or develop policies that will reconcile the requirements of human sympathy with the necessity for economic mobility. No democracy is now prepared to enforce the severe sanctions of bankruptcy and the Poor Law or even permit these capitalist incentives to operate as an effective threat. Any large and established group of employers or workers knows that it can command the legislative services of an elected assembly to protect it from serious hardship. The social conscience of a prosperous democratic community will no longer tolerate the selection, by impersonal economic forces, of large numbers of individuals for unmerited punishment without attempting, however ineffectively, to aid them. The problem is to combine this perfectly proper development of our moral judgment with a strengthening, rather than a weakening, of the forces drawing men and women into more useful employments. The difficulty is purely administrative— to bring into existence the necessary facilities for training and directing recruitment and for rewarding equilibrating movement. A control of the location of industry and powers to influence the rate of recruitment to depressed industries would go a long way to make the problem soluble. There is no reason why the abandonment of suffering as the chief method of inducing desirable change should leave us empty of devices for promoting mobility; in almost all fields of social discipline rewards have proved more powerful incentives than punishments.

In any case there is no ground for economists to prefer restriction to adaptation.

In the fourth place, very few economists are opposed to the further extension of the productive social services—education, health and the rehabilitation of the unemployed. They are able to appreciate, more clearly than other people, the importance of maintaining and increasing the skill and health of the population and the necessity for directing investment into human capital in the absence of any commercial motive for doing so.

8 It may be thought that all this amounts to very little and that the ground of agreement between economists, if this is all there is to it, is too restricted to be of any value.

I do not feel that this is so for two reasons. In the first place, the principles of agreement are not unimportant. If economists could emphasise the weight they attach to investment policy, to financial co-operation between the nations, to the practice of more humane methods of moving capital and labour from industry to industry, and to a further extension of the productive social services, I believe that the laity would be surprised, interested and even inspired. Nor would the practical consequences be wholly negligible. If the agreed policies were vigorously pursued, and if the accepted theories upon which they are based are correct, then it should prove possible to reduce cyclical unemployment very greatly, to abolish violent fluctuations in the foreign exchanges, to resume international lending on a large scale, to bring a new and painless power of adaptation into the distribution of industrial resources, to secure equality of opportunity and a happier and more productive community. These achievements, though modest in comparison with those of which a rational society would be capable, are not to be sneezed at. Economists would have done something to earn their living if, by agreement, they had instructed the imagination and inspired the will of their fellow citizens to this modest programme of improvement.

In the second place, I believe the field of agreement would widen as it was cultivated. We should discover that the victories of dialectic are pyrrhic, that the rewards of a common search for truth are more fruitful, more enduring. We should find crystallising under our feet, out of the present quagmires of dispute and speculation, the secure foundation of verified (or modified) hypotheses.

After years of neglect we are presented with a great opportunity. The opinions of economists, for the first time in thirty years, are given almost too much weight in the counsels of the nation. It is to be hoped that we shall not, through vanity, fail to make use of it.

INDEX

Index

Index

For Product Safety Concerns and Information please contact our EU
representative GPSR@taylorandfrancis.com Taylor & Francis Verlag GmbH,
Kaufingerstraße 24, 80331 München, Germany

Printed and bound by CPI Group (UK) Ltd, Croydon, CR0 4YY
08/05/2025
01864422-0001